THIS IS INDIANA

TOM CREAN, THE TEAM, AND THE EXCITING COMEBACK OF HOOSIER BASKETBALL

THE HERALD-TIMES
INDIANA UNIVERSITY PRESS
BLOOMINGTON

THIS IS
INDIANA

The Herald-Times

Photographs by Chris Howell

This book is a publication of

Indiana University Press
601 North Morton Street
Bloomington, Indiana 47404-3797 USA

iupress.indiana.edu

Telephone orders 800-842-6796
Fax orders 812-855-7931

Contents

CONTENTS

Before the 2011-2012 Indiana University men's basketball season began, optimistic Hoosier fans talked of a return to a post-season tournament. The wreckage from Kelvin Sampson running the program off the rails, with NCAA violations and players who didn't fit into the Indiana tradition, was cleaned up and the train was about to be back on track.

The buildup went like this: coach Tom Crean willed his undermanned team to six victories in the 2008-2009 season; to 10 in the following year; and to 12 in the 2010-2011 campaign. Surely the Hoosiers, with new recruit Cody Zeller and almost the rest of the team back from the previous seasons, could get the four or five more victories necessary to be playing in a tournament in March of 2012.

When Crean was introduced in 2008 as the coach who could bring IU back, he said he wanted the job for one reason. "It's Indiana," he said. "It's Indiana."

Indiana is one of college basketball's most storied programs. It's expected to be playing in the NCAA tournament every year. But it hadn't been close for the last three years. The optimists thought the Hoosiers would make it back for sure in the 2013 season, hoping for a moderate step to say, the NIT, in 2012. Then some things started to click.

IU won a road game at North Carolina State. Then came The Shot for a new generation — Christian Watford's game-winner on Dec. 10 against No. 1 Kentucky in Assembly Hall.

Fans started to believe because, to paraphrase Crean, This is Indiana. Twelve victories were in the books before the Big Ten season began. After a loss in the Big Ten opener at Michigan State came a New Year's Eve win over No. 2 Ohio State.

Zeller was as good as advertised, possibly better. And others stepped up to play key roles: Sophomores Victor Oladipo and Will Sheehey brought energy and athleticism; juniors Christian Watford and Jordan Hulls brought consistent scoring and experienced play; junior Derek Elston and seniors Verdell Jones III, Tom Pritchard and Matt Roth brought key contributions, such as a deflection, a crucial assist or mid-range jumper, a big offensive rebound or a deep 3-point shot.

After a loss at Michigan on Feb. 1, the Hoosiers were 17-6 overall, 5-6 in the Big Ten. The post-season was assured, but with several tough games ahead the NCAA Tournament was still in question.

A big victory came three days later at Purdue, then two more at home to gain the 20-win mark. A loss at Iowa stalled the momentum, before IU reeled off four straight victories to finish the regular season 24-7. A return to the NCAA was guaranteed.

The night of the pairings, critics started to surface again. IU's first opponent, New Mexico State, was touted by some as likely to upset the Hoosiers. Didn't happen. Then tournament darling VCU was the trendy pick to knock off IU. Sheehey's jump-shot from the baseline sealed a two-point victory for the Hoosiers.

An estimated 500 people met the Hoosiers when they returned to Bloomington. They wanted to pay tribute to the players and coaches who had brought IU back from the turmoil that began four years before. The Hoosiers were headed to the Sweet 16.

A rematch with No. 1 Kentucky was next, and although the Hoosiers lost that one, 102-90, there was no doubt: IU was back.

Herald-Times sports writer Dustin Dopirak and photographer Chris Howell covered every game, as well as everything that happened before the season and between games. Some of their work is packaged here to help fans remember this special season … and to put an exclamation point on what this team said to the college basketball world:

This is Indiana!

BOB ZALTSBERG
EDITOR
THE HERALD-TIMES

THIS IS INDIANA

Indiana Hoosiers forward
Cody Zeller (40) tries to lay
the ball in as Evansville Aces
guard/forward Kenneth Harris
(32) defends during the Indiana
Evansville basketball game
at the Ford Center in
Evansville, Ind.,
Wednesday, Nov. 16, 2011.

"New" Hoosiers Come Up Aces

IU routs Evansville for 1st road victory in more than a season

By Dustin Dopirak

After Indiana's surgical evisceration of Evansville on Wednesday night, the question posed to Tom Crean and his players sounded like a reasonable one.

In Crean's four years, the Hoosiers had won games by bigger margins and earned victories of much more gravity against much stronger teams. But those more important victories were mostly nailbiters, and none of those blowouts came against a team as respectable as this Evansville squad, which was coming off a 16-16 season in the revered Missouri Valley Conference and a season opening win over Butler.

So was IU's 94-73 win at Evansville in front of 9,640 at the brand new Ford Center the Hoosiers' best all-around performance in Crean's three-plus years of rebuilding?

Senior guard Verdell Jones III, who has been with Crean for all 30 of his previous wins at IU and all 66 of his losses, says yes.

"I think so," Jones said. "On the defensive end and on the offensive end, the first half was really good."

Crean refused to take the bait.

"This is a new team," Crean said. "This is a new team. It's a new year."

After Wednesday's performance, he will receive very little argument with that.

Winning on the road provided significant proof of that. Before Wednesday, the Hoosiers (3-0) had won just one true road game in Crean's tenure, and it was at Penn State on Jan. 21, 2010. At no point in Crean's previous three years have the Hoosiers displayed this much firepower, nor have they been able to put this many dangerous scorers on the floor at once. They certainly haven't had a post presence like Cody Zeller.

Evansville couldn't handle any of that Wednesday night. Indiana had five scorers in double figures and junior forward Derek Elston was one point away from making it six. The Hoosiers made 10 of their first 12 field goal attempts and 18 of their first 26. They shot 55.9 percent (33-of-59) from the field as a team, and made 51.9 percent of their buckets in the second half even though the starters watched most of it from the bench.

"It was great," Jones said. "You couldn't key on one guy. I think it all started with getting the ball to the big fella right here in Cody. He was just making plays. They were double-teaming and he was kicking it and we were driving and kicking it. It was good thing to have Cody command a double team like that."

After admittedly having trouble playing through the post in preseason practice, the Hoosiers seem to be developing more of an appreciation for Zeller's ability to move the ball, and it showed Wednesday. Zeller with finished with 14 points on 6-for-7 shooting and nine rebounds, and as Jones said, his presence opened up driving space in the lane and room on the perimeter.

Jones led all scorers with 17 points, knocking down a career-high four 3-pointers, and also had seven assists. Junior guard Jordan Hulls had 14 points, while sophomore swingman Will Sheehey added 10. Sophomore guard Victor Oladipo had eight points and four assists, mostly on drive-and-kicks to Jones in the corners. Junior swingman Christian Watford, meanwhile, had his best performance of the season after slinking to a combined nine points on 3-of-14 shooting in the season's first two games. Watford battled an Achilles tendon injury for most of the preseason, but he seemed much healthier on Wednesday, hitting 5-of-7 shots for 15 points to go with eight rebounds.

"I got it going tonight," Watford said. "My teammates have been helping me do a great job keeping my head up and stuff like that even when times have been tough. I've been struggling."

The Hoosiers' offense also fed off the defense. Evansville shot 51.9 percent in a garbage time to finish at 42.9 percent for the game, but IU held the Aces (1-1) to just 34.5 percent in the first half.

They also did a number on Evansville star guard Colt Ryan. With Oladipo draped on Ryan and consistent help defense behind him, Ryan shot 1-for-6 in the first half and scored just four points. He finished with 17 on 4-of-10 shooting, but by the time he found a rhythm, Evansville had no chance of a comeback.

"There's no doubt that our guys were locked in," Crean said. "I thought our defensive intensity and intelligence combined were really, really good. Really good. When you go on the road, everything's gotta turn up a notch."

It was obvious from the beginning that it did, as IU took an 11-3 lead out of the break and never again let Evansville get closer than six points.

Evansville cut a 13-point Indiana lead to 31-23 with 8:01 to go in the first half, but IU finished the half on a 20-6 run to take a 51-27 advantage into the break. They toyed with the Aces in the second half, but still got to comfortably enjoy victory on someone else's floor for the first time in almost 22 months.

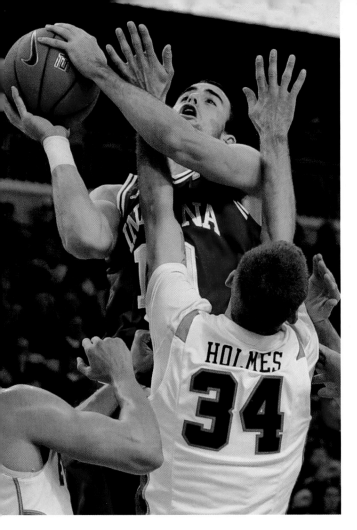

(Above) Indiana Hoosiers guard Jordan Hulls (1) saves the loose ball as Evansville Aces guard/forward Colt Ryan (11) defends during the Indiana Evansville basketball game.

(Left) Indiana Hoosiers guard/forward Will Sheehey (10) shoots over Evansville Aces guard/forward Denver Holmes (34).

(Below) Head coach Tom Crean points out the time left on the shot clock.

INDIANA 94

	Min	3PFG	AFG	FT	O-R	A	PF	Pts
Watford, f	24	2-3	5-7	3-3	0-8	1	0	15
Zeller, f	26	0-0	6-7	2-3	1-9	1	4	14
Hulls, g	27	2-3	5-7	2-2	0-0	2	2	14
Oladipo, g	24	0-2	3-8	2-4	2-4	4	4	8
Jones, g	25	4-4	5-8	3-5	2-5	7	2	17
Barnett	1	0-0	0-0	0-0	0-0	0	0	0
Sheehey	21	1-4	3-8	3-5	0-2	2	1	10
DMoore	11	0-0	0-2	0-0	1-2	4	2	0
Etherington	4	0-0	0-0	0-0	0-1	2	0	0
Smith	1	0-0	0-1	0-0	0-0	0	0	0
Abell	7	0-1	1-3	2-3	0-0	1	0	4
Howard	1	0-0	0-0	0-0	0-0	0	1	0
Pritchard	6	0-0	0-0	0-0	0-1	1	1	0
Roth	6	1-2	1-2	0-0	0-0	0	0	3
Elston	17	1-2	4-6	0-0	1-3	1	3	9
team					2-2			
Totals		11-21	33-59	17-25	9-37	24	22	94
Shooting		.524	.559	.680				

EVANSVILLE 73

	Min	3PFG	AFG	FT	O-R	A	PF	Pts
Harris, f	24	1-1	5-10	6-7	0-4	0	3	17
Holmes, f	33	2-4	5-8	1-2	0-1	3	4	13
Peeler, c	8	0-0	0-1	0-0	0-1	0	2	0
Taylor, g	26	0-0	1-4	2-2	0-3	5	5	4
Ryan, g	33	3-4	4-10	6-9	1-5	1	4	17
Nelson	8	1-2	2-3	0-0	0-1	0	0	5
Jones	17	0-2	2-4	1-3	0-0	0	4	5
JMoore	3	0-0	0-0	0-0	0-0	0	0	0
Jahr	13	0-1	2-5	0-0	1-4	0	1	4
Cox	22	0-0	2-9	1-2	4-5	2	1	4
Cesnlvisius	13	0-0	1-2	2-2	4-2	5	1	4
team					3-6			
Totals		7-16	24-56	18-27	10-32	12	25	73
Shooting		.438	.429	.667				

Indiana (3-0)		51	43—94
Evansville (1-1)		27	46—73

Blocks: Indiana 5 (Zeller 2, Jones 2, Sheehey), Evansville 5 (Cesnulevisius, Harris, Holmes, Peeler, Ryan). **Turnovers:** Indiana 12 (Zeller 3, Jones 3, Hulls 2, Oladipo 2, Watford, Sheehey), Evansville 16 (Harris 2, Peeler 2, Taylor 2, Ryan 2, Jones 2, Cox 2, Holmes, Nelson, Jahr, Cesnulevisius). **Steals:** Indiana 7 (Oladipo 3, Watford, Zeller, Hulls, Moore), Evansville 5 (Harris 2, Taylor 2, Holmes). **Officials:** Mike Sanzere, Tom Eades, Paul Janssen. **A:** 9,640.

Evansville Aces guard Ned Cox (22) drives the lane on Indiana Hoosiers guard Verdell Jones III (12) .

Indiana Hoosiers forward Christian Watford (2) is fouled by Butler Bulldogs forward Khyle Marshall (23) as he attempts to dunk the ball during the Indiana Butler men's basketball game at Assembly Hall in Bloomington, Ind., Sunday, Nov. 27, 2011.

IU Will-ed to Victory

Sheehey's career-high 21 points lead Hoosiers to 75-59 win over Butler

By Dustin Dopirak

It is standard procedure to describe sixth men as catalysts, to speak of them providing sparks or injections of energy and scoring.

But as much as Indiana sophomore swingman and first man off the bench Will Sheehey sparked the Hoosiers on Sunday night, he also steadied them during what was unquestionably the most turbulent stretch of basketball the Hoosiers have played this year. In large part because of Sheehey, the Hoosiers never trailed during a slump of 10 minutes and 21 seconds without a field goal. He finished with a career-high 21 points, helping Indiana hold off a gritty Butler squad and run away with a 75-59 win in front of 17,265 at Assembly Hall on Sunday night.

The game served as the de facto championship game of the Hoosier Invitational, a round-robin event that included IU, Butler, Chattanooga, Savannah State and Gardner-Webb but did not have a tournament setup. Indiana (6-0) claimed a trophy for the victory, however, and Sheehey was named tournament MVP.
"Will really did a great job of reading the game," Indiana coach Tom Crean said. "… He's got some real innate ability to read situations."

And the situation, as Sheehey read it, was that Sunday night's game was brutally physical and slightly manic. Both teams were stingy on defense and trying to play fast, which led to lots of turnovers and fouls. He saw them as opportunities.
"They're very aggressive on ball screens, as you saw," Sheehey said. "Every time someone came off the screen, they showed the big really long. On the weak side of the floor, there was a lot of open things. … And also, in transition, they brought a lot of guys to the board as you can see, they had I don't know how many offensive rebounds. When they go to the boards, there's a lot of leak outs and dunks and what not."

Sheehey mostly took advantage during the period when Indiana most needed any sort of offense. From the 8:28 mark of the first half to the 11:43 mark of the second half, the Hoosiers, who were shooting 57.1 percent from the field coming into the game, managed just six field goals. Sheehey had three of those and assisted on a fourth. He also went to the line three times in that period and knocked down 5 of 6 free throws.
Sheehey finished 5-for-8 from the field and 8-for-10 from the free-throw line. He hit a career-high three 3-pointers on four attempts. He had hit just 2 of 7 in the Hoosiers' first five games and 7 of 23 all last season.

Just as important as that was what he did on defense. Hopkins was 6-for-11 in the first half for 13 points, with sophomore guard Victor Oladipo and Sheehey alternating on the assignment. Sheehey wanted it in the second half, though, and with the help of IU's big men switching screens, he held Hopkins to just one field goal in the final 20 minutes. Hopkins didn't even attempt a field goal in the last 18:54 and finished with 19 points.
"Will wanted the matchup," Crean said. "That's something we're very comfortable with, but he went in there and did something with it."

Sheehey's performance on Hopkins was just part of a strong overall defensive effort by the Hoosiers, who held Butler (3-3) to 38.2 percent shooting, including just 5-for-18 (27.8 percent) from the 3-point line. Sophomore forward Khyle Marshall added 16 points, but no one else for Butler had more than six. The Hoosiers caused 21 turnovers and scored 23 points off of them.
"I'm blown away by our defensive effort," Crean said. "We kept bringing it defensively. We kept getting to the 50-50s. As I told the team, I think you got better in the game, but I know you got tougher. And that's a big, big deal."

After shooting just 32 percent (8-for-25) in the first half, Indiana shot 50 percent (11-for-22) in the second half.

Sheehey was one of four Hoosiers to score in double figures. Freshman forward Cody Zeller had his worst shooting game (4-for-9) and struggled to get room while being defended by Butler's Andrew Smith but still finished with 16 points and eight rebounds. Junior guard Jordan Hulls had 14 points and three assists, and Oladipo managed 10 points and seven rebounds.

The Hoosiers led by just three points (40-37) with 12:15 to go, but went on a quick 11-2 run to take a 51-39 advantage at the 9:29 mark. Butler would cut the deficit to 51-43, but Indiana answered with a 20-8 spurt to take a 20-point lead with 2:08 remaining, turning a turbulent game into a convincing win.

BUTLER 59

	Min	3PFG	AFG	FT	O-R	A	PF	Pts
Butcher, f	14	0- 1	0- 4	0- 2	5- 6	0	0	0
Smith, c	29	1- 5	1- 7	0- 0	2- 7	0	1	3
Nored, g	28	0- 1	1- 5	4- 6	1- 3	2	3	6
Hopkins, g	29	1- 3	7-12	4- 4	0- 2	0	4	19
Stigall, g	24	1- 4	2- 6	1- 3	0- 0	1	5	6
Barlow	1	0- 0	0- 0	0- 0	0- 0	0	0	0
Fromm	6	0- 1	0- 2	1- 3	1- 1	0	1	1
Aldridge	19	1- 2	1- 4	0- 0	0- 1	1	1	3
Jones	20	0- 0	2- 6	1- 2	2- 5	2	4	5
Marshall	28	1- 1	7- 9	1- 2	1- 4	1	2	16
Kampen	1	0- 0	0- 0	0- 0	0- 0	0	0	0
Woods	1	0- 0	0- 0	0- 0	1- 1	0	1	0
team					3-4			
Totals		5-18	21-55	12-22	16-34	7	22	59
Shooting		.278	.382	.545				

INDIANA 75

	Min	3PFG	AFG	FT	O-R	A	PF	Pts
Watford, f	20	1- 2	2-10	2- 4	2- 2	1	2	7
Zeller, f	33	0- 0	4- 9	8-10	3- 8	0	2	16
Hulls, g	38	2- 3	5- 9	2- 2	1- 2	3	2	14
Oladipo, g	26	1- 2	2- 5	5- 6	2- 7	0	4	10
Jones, g	18	0- 0	0- 3	2- 2	2- 4	1	3	2
Barnett	1	0- 0	0- 0	0- 0	0- 0	0	0	0
Sheehey	31	3- 4	5- 8	8-10	1- 3	2	2	21
Moore	3	0- 0	0- 0	0- 0	0- 0	1	0	0
Pritchard	9	0- 0	0- 0	0- 0	0- 0	0	0	0
Roth	7	1- 2	1- 2	2- 2	0- 1	0	0	5
Elston	14	0- 0	0- 1	0- 0	0- 2	1	3	0
team					1-7			
Totals		8-13	19-47	29-36	12-36	9	18	75
Shooting		.615	.404	.806				

(Above, Left) Indiana Hoosiers guard Jordan Hulls (1) and Indiana Hoosiers guard Victor Oladipo (4) celebrate taking a double digit lead during the Indiana Butler men's basketball game.

(Left) Butler Bulldogs guard Chase Stigall (33) fouls Indiana Hoosiers forward Cody Zeller (40) .

Butler (3-3)	28	31	59
Indiana (6-0)	31	44	75

Blocks: Butler 4 (Smith 2, Butcher, Marshall), Indiana 6 (Watford 2, Zeller 2, Oladipo, Pritchard). **Turnovers:** Butler 21 (Hopkins 7, Smith 4, Nored 2, Stigall 2, Woods 2, team 2, Aldridge, Marshall), Indiana 16 (Watford 3, Oladipo 3, Jones 3, Sheehey 3, Hulls 2, Zeller, Elston). **Steals:** Butler 13 (Nored 5, Smith 2, Butcher, Stigall, Barlow, Aldridge, Jones, Woods), Indiana 14 (Zeller 3, Hulls 2, Oladipo 2, Sheehey 2, Moore 2, Pritchard 2, Elston). **Officials:** John Higgins, Joe DeRosa, Jamie Luckie. **A:** 17,265.

(Above) Indiana Hoosiers guard Verdell Jones III (12) throws the ball back in as he falls out of bounds and Butler Bulldogs guard Chase Stigall (33) defends.

(Right) Indiana Hoosiers forward Cody Zeller (40) shows his disappointment after a foul was called.

Indiana Hoosiers guard Victor Oladipo (4) gets his fourth foul attempting to block the shot of North Carolina State Wolfpack forward Richard Howell (1) as Indiana Hoosiers forward Cody Zeller (40) helps defend during the Indiana North Carolina State men's basketball game in Raleigh, N.C., Wednesday, Nov. 30, 2011. Indiana won 86-75.

IU posts 'monumental' win

Hoosiers put away N.C. State for first Challenge victory under Crean, 86-75

By Dustin Dopirak

For a brief moment once the buzzer sounded, Christian Watford allowed himself to celebrate like it was March.

He corralled a pass around midcourt, took a couple high and hard dribbles and then flung the ball high toward the overhead scoreboard as he bounded toward the Indiana bench and did a few flying leaps into his teammates.

After that, the Hoosiers toned down the exuberance for the handshake line with North Carolina State, reminding themselves that there were still a few hours left in November. But they were still bouncing as they hit the tunnel after beating the Wolfpack 86-75 in front of 16,597 at the RBC Center, though, because they knew exactly how big this win was.

It was the Hoosiers' first win in the ACC/Big Ten Challenge in coach Tom Crean's tenure, with the last coming against Georgia Tech under Kelvin Sampson in 2007. It was Indiana's second road victory this season, but its first outside the state since it won at Penn State on Jan. 21, 2010. It was also the Hoosiers' first win over a power six conference team this year, and the clearest indication yet that their 7-0 start could be legitimate.

"It's monumental for this program," Crean said. "We've never won in this game, OK, and we hadn't been to an atmosphere like this. … It's a landmark win for us as a program. It's certainly one of the bigger wins in our time without a doubt, because we played a really good team in a great atmosphere, a sold-out atmosphere. We had to figure out different ways to win it."

Which made it even bigger.

It was the first time this season the Hoosiers had to beat a team that was at worst even and arguably superior to them in terms of size and athleticism. It was also the first time they had to overcome a significant second-half deficit to do it, as they trailed by seven points with 7:48 to go.

"We learned that if we stay together, we could accomplish anything," Watford said. "At that point, when we were down seven, we didn't give up. We knew we had it. We were calm and we knew what it needed to be. So we just kept fighting."

They pulled it off because of contributions from across the board. Junior point guard Jordan Hulls gave arguably his most commanding leadership performance as a college player. He led the team with 20 points, dished out five assists and hit three 3-pointers. He hit all five of his free throws, extending his school record

streak to 52, and one of his 3-pointers was arguably the shot of the game. He came off a pick and roll and drilled one late in the shot clock to give Indiana a 79-75 advantage with 1:38 to go, and North Carolina State never recovered.

Freshman forward Cody Zeller had 19 points and seven rebounds, with 13 of the points and five of the rebounds coming in a dominant second half. Many of those points came after Zeller's parents left to see his older brother Tyler play at North Carolina. "Tough luck," Zeller deadpanned to laughter in the press room. "Maybe they shouldn't have come at all. We would've won by 20." Watford, meanwhile broke out of a funk that carried over from his 2-for-10 performance against Butler on Sunday through the first half. The junior swingman recorded 11 of his 16 points and seven of his nine rebounds in the second half.

"He hit huge shots for us," Hulls said. "Got to the rim, got to the free throw line. We know what C-Wat's capable of when he puts his mind to it. He did that for us, that's really why he won the game. He got huge rebounds at the end of the game."

So did others, which allowed the Hoosiers to correct their biggest first half deficiency. They were down 22-13 on the boards at halftime, with the long-armed North Carolina State squad grabbing 13 offensive boards and turning them into 16 second-chance points, a big part of the reason the Wolfpack (5-2) led 42-41 at the break.

In the second half, the Hoosiers won the battle of the boards, 24-18. Even when the Indiana fell behind 63-56 with 7:48 left, Crean said he wasn't worried because he saw more fight on the glass. "Maybe the calmest I was all night was when we had I think it was three straight shots in the basket on offensive rebounds," Crean said. "It looked like volleyball on the boards, but at least we were in there. Timeout came and I said, 'We're finally here. We're finally playing.' I looked up at the score and we were down seven and it was the biggest deficit we had, but it was like we were finally playing the game the way it needed to be played."

The Hoosiers had squandered a 25-14 start and the Wolfpack were on a 7-0 run at the time, but the Hoosiers turned the game around and never looked back. They outscored North Carolina State 30-12 from that point and 10-0 in the last 1:38 to clinch this squad's biggest win to date.

INDIANA 86

	Min	3PFG	AFG	FT	O-R	A	PF	Pts
Watford, f	33	3-5	4-9	5-6	2-9	0	2	16
Zeller, c	31	0-0	8-14	3-4	5-7	0	2	19
Hulls, g	36	3-4	6-9	5-5	1-4	5	2	20
Oladipo, g	22	0-1	4-12	3-4	1-3	0	4	11
Jones, g	27	0-0	3-6	1-1	0-2	2	2	7
Sheehey	23	0-1	3-7	2-3	2-6	1	2	8
Abell	8	1-1	2-4	0-0	0-1	1	0	5
Pritchard	9	0-0	0-0	0-0	0-2	0	3	0
Roth	3	0-0	0-0	0-0	0-0	0	0	1
Elston	8	0-1	0-1	0-0	0-0	0	0	1
team					0-3			
Totals		7-13	30-62	19-23	12-37	8	20	86
Shooting		.538	.484	.826				

N.C. STATE 75

	Min	3PFG	AFG	FT	O-R	A	PF	Pts
Howell, f	20	0-0	3-6	0-0	3-6	0	3	6
Wood, f	39	3-4	4-8	5-5	1-2	1	5	16
Painter, c	27	0-0	5-13	0-0	3-6	1	2	10
Brown, g	35	0-1	6-13	7-9	1-6	5	1	19
Williams, g	24	0-1	4-9	0-0	5-5	3	3	8
Johnson	10	0-3	1-4	2-2	0-1	2	0	4
Leslie	33	0-1	4-11	2-3	3-11	1	4	10
Harris	12	0-0	1-2	0-0	0-0	1	1	2
team					2-3			
Totals		3-10	28-66	16-22	18-40	14	19	75
Shooting		.300	.424	.727				

Indiana (7-0)		41	45—86
N.C. State (5-2)		42	33—75

Blocks: Indiana 4 (Zeller 2, Watford, Oladipo), N.C. State 10 (Leslie 3, Painter 2, Wood 2, Williams 2, Brown). **Turnovers:** Indiana 13 (Jones 3, Sheehey 3, Watford 2, Hulls 2, Oladipo, Zeller, Roth), N.C. State 15 (Leslie 5, Howell 4, Brown 3, Painter, Wood, Johnson). **Steals:** Indiana 10 (Oladipo 3, Jones 3, Hulls 2, Zeller, Abell), N.C. State (7 (Howell 2, Painter, Brown, Williams, Leslie, Harris). **Officials:** Bryan Kersey, Roger Ayers, Earl Watson. **A:** 16,597.

(Right) Indiana Hoosiers forward Christian Watford (2) shoots to help pull the Hoosiers away with the lead late in the second half during the Indiana North Carolina State men's basketball game.

(Opposite page, left) Indiana Hoosiers guard Victor Oladipo (4) is fouled by North Carolina State Wolfpack forward C.J. Leslie (5) after stealing the ball.

(Opposite page, right) Indiana Hoosiers forward Derek Elston (32) knocks the ball loose from North Carolina State Wolfpack guard Alex Johnson (3).

(Opposite page, center) Head coach Tom Crean hugs Indiana Hoosiers guard Victor Oladipo (4) as they leave the floor after the game.

(Opposite page, left) The Hoosier bench cheers their starters.

Indiana Hoosiers forward Christian Watford (2) hits the game winning last second shot over Kentucky Wildcats guard Darius Miller (1) during the Indiana Kentucky men's basketball game at Assembly Hall in Bloomington, Ind., Saturday, Dec. 10, 2011. Indiana won 73-72.

'It Was a Great Feeling'

Watford's 3-pointer at horn lifts IU over No. 1 UK, 73-72

By Dustin Dopirak

Within seconds of his picture-perfect, buzzer-beating 3-pointer's contact with the net on Assembly Hall's north goal, Christian Watford was prone on the floor and swimming in an ocean of human catharsis.

The Indiana student section didn't so much storm the court after the Hoosiers stunned No. 1 Kentucky, 73-72, as swallow it whole. The mayhem built outward from the spot where Watford fell on the floor near the scorer's table on the west sideline and kept getting bigger until fans covered every single wood panel on Branch McCracken Court at Assembly Hall from end to end.

Fans were singing along with the pep band and lifting each other on their shoulders and trying to find players and coaches to whom to express their gratitude. Watford and several of his teammates escaped from beneath the crush of humanity only to bathe in its glow, standing atop the scorer's table and gesturing to the crowd as if directing some joyful orchestra.

"It was a great feeling," Watford said. "I haven't felt anything like that. That's probably the most memorable moment of my life. It's the biggest shot, definitely, of my career."

And it was the biggest thing, definitely, that's happened to Indiana since the program was decimated following Kelvin Sampson's 2008 recruiting scandal and the subsequent roster purge that left the Hoosiers with just two returning players in coach Tom Crean's first season.

IU fans suffered through seasons of pain and defeat since then, as the Hoosiers didn't even come close to .500 in any of those seasons and went a combined 28-66. They drained the marrow from any and all brief moments of joy in that time. Last season, the student section somewhat reluctantly rushed the court for a win over an Illinois team that was ranked No. 20 at the time — a move that would've been considered unthinkable before 2008 but seemed justifiable at the time.

On Saturday, they packed Assembly Hall with a capacity crowd of 17,472 hoping not just for an upset and a victory over a hated rival, but proof that Indiana was back. They got the most irrefutable evidence they could hope to receive in the month of December.

The Hoosiers defeated the No. 1 team in the country for the first time since beating Duke in the 2002 NCAA Tournament and was the first such win at Assembly Hall since Kirk Haston's buzzer beater took down top-ranked Michigan State in 2001. IU's first win over Kentucky since 2007 gave them a 9-0 start for the first

time since the 1989-90 season and puts them in position to return to the Top 25 for the first time 2008.

"This is one of the most shared moments that I've ever been a part of," Crean said afterward, his hair still wet after his team doused him with a Gatorade bucket filled with water in the locker room. "Maybe the most shared moment, where you want to share it with everybody that's been a part of this program long before we got here. … It's one of those moments that everybody's gonna remember."

Watford led all scorers with 20 points in the game, hitting four of six 3-pointers and also holding Kentucky forward Terrence Jones, a preseason All-American, to just four points. IU sophomore guard Victor Oladipo had 13 points. Freshman forward Cody Zeller and junior guard Jordan Hulls had 11 points each, and sophomore swingman Will Sheehey added 10.

There was a period late in the game when it appeared the Hoosiers would remember Saturday's game not because they won, but because they had the game in their grasp and lost it.

After taking a 30-29 advantage at the end of a choppy first half that included a combined 24 turnovers between the two teams, the Hoosiers caught fire from outside early in the second half and took a 10-point advantage.

But the Wildcats' world-class athleticism and length eventually got them back into it. Though star freshman forward Anthony Davis was on the bench with foul trouble, and Watford had rendered Jones largely ineffective, the Wildcats still had plenty of weapons. They attacked off the dribble with point guard Marquis Teague and shooting guard Doron Lamb and with post-feeds to swingmen Darius Miller and Michael Kidd-Gilchrist. Lamb had 19 points, Kidd-Gilchrist 18 and Teague 15, helping Kentucky shoot 68 percent in the second half.

With two minutes to go, Kentucky took the lead on a dunk by Miller. IU took it back on a driving layup by Watford, but Teague drove to the bucket to make it 71-70 with 49 seconds to go.

After Watford missed a jumper, Kentucky freshman forward Anthony Davis missed the front end of a one-and-one with 19 seconds left, and Indiana was hoping to hold the ball for the last shot, but Oladipo lost possession on a drive from the right wing, and the Hoosiers had to foul Lamb. Lamb only made one of two free throws, however, giving the Hoosiers the ball with 5.6 seconds to go and a chance to tie or take the lead with a 3.

Watford inbounded the ball to senior guard Verdell Jones III, who wasn't defended until almost midcourt, where Teague tried to foul him — Kentucky had two to give before the bonus — but missed while being screened by Zeller. Jones took the ball over to the left wing, stopped and flipped the ball out to Watford for the open 3. The ball found the net just as the buzzer went off.

"The plan was to get a basket, get a 2 and go to overtime," Jones said. "But big-time players make big-time plays, and C-Wat did. When I got the ball, I knew he was going to be sprinting down, because he was taking the ball out. He was sprinting behind and he was trailing me. I just drove it and he was like, 'V!' 'V!' I just turned around and passed it to him, and the rest was history."

And more than three years of Indiana catharsis flooding onto the Assembly Hall floor.

(Below) Indiana Hoosiers forward Cody Zeller (40) and Indiana Hoosiers guard Jordan Hulls (1) celebrate with the Hoosier fans after the game.

Indiana Hoosiers guard Jordan Hulls (1) hits a 3-pointer over Kentucky Wildcats forward Michael Kidd-Gilchrist (14).

Indiana Hoosiers forward Christian Watford (2) was swarmed by Hoosier fans after hitting the game winning last second shot.

KENTUCKY 72

	Min	3PFG	AFG	FT	O-R	A	PF	Pts
Jones, f	28	0- 0	2- 3	0- 2	0- 1	1	0	4
K-Gilchrist, f	38	0- 0	9-12	0- 0	4- 9	0	1	18
Davis, c	24	0- 0	3- 4	0- 1	2- 9	1	4	6
Lamb, g	36	2- 3	5-14	7-11	1- 1	1	2	19
Teague, g	31	0- 1	6-11	3- 3	0- 1	5	2	15
Miller	26	0- 3	4- 8	0- 0	0- 2	0	3	8
Vargas	10	0- 0	1- 2	0- 0	2- 3	0	0	2
Wiltjer	7	0- 0	0- 0	0- 0	0- 0	1	1	0
team					1- 4			
Totals		2- 7	30-54	10-17	10-30	9	13	72
Shooting		.286	.556	.588				

INDIANA 73

	Min	3PFG	AFG	FT	O-R	A	PF	Pts
Watford, f	30	4- 6	8-15	0- 0	1- 5	1	5	20
Zeller, c	37	0- 0	4- 8	3- 3	5- 7	1	2	11
Hulls, g	35	3- 6	4- 7	0- 0	0- 0	2	5	11
Oladipo, g	32	0- 0	4-12	5- 6	3- 7	1	2	13
Jones, g	34	0- 1	2- 7	4- 5	2- 4	3	2	8
Sheehey	16	2- 2	3- 8	2- 2	1- 1	0	3	10
Moore	5	0- 0	0- 0	0- 0	1- 0	0	1	0
Pritchard	11	0- 0	0- 1	0- 0	0- 2	1	1	0
team					2- 2			
Totals		9-15	25-58	14-17	14-30	12	16	73
Shooting		.600	.431	.824				

Kentucky (81)		29	43—72
Indiana (9-0)		30	43—73

Blocks: Kentucky 6 (Jones 2, Kidd-Gilchrist 2, Davis, Lamb), Indiana 2 (Zeller, Oladipo). **Turnovers:** Kentucky 17 (Jones 6, Teague 3, Kidd-Gilchrist 2, Miller 2, Davis, Lamb, Wiltjer, team), Indiana 18 (Hulls 5, Jones 5, Zeller 3, Oladipo 3, Watford, Pritchard). **Steals:** Kentucky 10 (Davis 3, Kidd-Gilchrist 2, Lamb 2, Jones, Teague, Vargas), Indiana 7 (Hulls 4, Watford, Zeller, Jones). **Officials:** Ted Valentine, Mike Kitts, Tom Eades. **A:** 17,472.

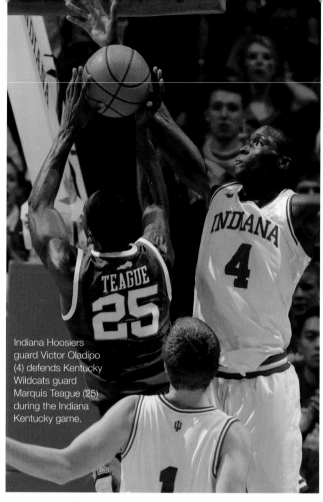

Indiana Hoosiers guard Victor Oladipo (4) defends Kentucky Wildcats guard Marquis Teague (25) during the Indiana Kentucky game.

Indiana Hoosiers forward Christian Watford (2) shoots over Kentucky Wildcats forward Terrence Jones (3) and Kentucky Wildcats forward Anthony Davis (23).

Indiana Hoosiers forward Cody Zeller (40) tries putting back the rebound over Kentucky Wildcats forward Anthony Davis (23) and Kentucky Wildcats forward Terrence Jones (3).

Indiana Hoosiers forward Christian Watford (2) was swarmed by Hoosier fans after hitting the game winning last second shot during the Indiana Kentucky men's basketball game at Assembly Hall in Bloomington, Ind., Saturday, Dec. 10, 2011. Indiana won 73-72.

Indiana Hoosiers guard Victor Oladipo (4) drives the ball on Notre Dame Fighting Irish guard Jerian Grant (22) during the Indiana Notre Dame men's basketball game at Conseco Fieldhouse in game two of the Close the Gap Crossroads Classic in Indianapolis, Ind., Saturday, Dec. 17, 2011.

Ugly Win for Hoosiers

IU beats Notre Dame, 69-58, to go 10-0 for first time since 1989-90 season

By Dustin Dopirak

Tom Crean doesn't know what Derek Elston was thinking, and it's hard to imagine anyone else could come up with a logical explanation either.

With the Hoosiers in a mad dash to get the ball down the floor for one more shot at the end of the first half of Saturday's game against Notre Dame, Elston pulled up from about half-court for a desperation heave. That would've been fine if there weren't 4.5 seconds still left on the clock.

But on a play that was strangely indicative of Indiana's entire day, freshman guard Remy Abell bolted under the bucket and put back Elston's wild miss at the buzzer to give Indiana a 26-20 lead at the half.

"Maybe he saw what Christian (Watford) saw last week with 0.8," Crean said, referring to Watford's buzzer-beater that knocked off No. 1 Kentucky. "I don't know. It looked more to me like it said 4.5 or somewhere in there, and he didn't see that. But the presence of mind of Remy was just fantastic."

Abell's effort was an example of the mindset the Hoosiers had throughout a 69-58 victory at Conseco Fieldhouse in the inaugural Crossroads Classic. They kept fighting, no matter what wasn't clicking or what went wrong, and just kept finding a way in a grind-it-out slugfest in which neither team could consistently find an offensive flow. By defending well and pounding the ball in the paint to freshman forward Cody Zeller, the Hoosiers were able to hold off the Fighting Irish.

IU improved to 10-0 for the first time since the 1989-90 season and is the only unbeaten team in the Big Ten. No Indiana team has started 11-0 since 1975-76, the last Division I team to finish the season undefeated, and the Hoosiers will certainly be favored to match that 11-0 mark against Howard on Monday. They have won all but one of their games — the Kentucky game — by double digits.

"Shots weren't falling for us," said Zeller, who led all scorers with 21 points. "We weren't getting many easy buckets, but we just had to do the little things. We can always play good defense and rebound, so we put a big emphasis on that."

That was especially true after the game's first seven minutes, when Notre Dame opened on a 15-6 run. Sophomore swingman Alex Dragicevich hit three 3-pointers in the first 5:13, sophomore guard Eric Atkins scored on a fast break layup and the Irish hit four free throws.

But the Irish scored just five points the rest of the first half. An Atkins layup at 14:33 was Notre Dame's last field goal of the first half, and the Irish finished the period shooting just 4-for-20 from the field.

"It was just being there on the catch instead of letting them face up, shoot over you or whatever the case may be," Indiana junior Jordan Hulls said. "We just had better ball pressure, better defense, better help side, just a lot more active, I felt like, after those first five minutes or whatever.

"They screen a lot. You've gotta be aware, and if you're not aware, then they'll backdoor you too. We just had to be very conscious of what they were doing, and I felt like our team defense really picked up."

Crean made sure the Hoosiers were cognizant of Notre Dame's prowess beyond the 3-point arc. The Irish average 6 1/2 3-pointers per game and entered Saturday's contest with five players who had hit at least 12 this season. But after Dragicevich's third, the Irish got just one more — with 1:41 to go in the game.

Atkins led the Irish with 15 points. Sophomore guard Jerian Grant had 14 and junior forward Jack Cooley 12, but just two other players scored more than two. Dragicevich did not score again after the 14:47 mark of the first half.

"We knew we were playing a very good team," Crean said. "A team full of very good basketball players that could drive, cut, slash, but most importantly shoot. Especially the 3. And for them to go 32 minutes without a 3-point field goal says a lot about the way our defense rose to the challenge of guarding a team that shoots as well as they do."

The Hoosiers didn't shoot much better, especially in the first half, but they took that as a mandate to get the ball to Zeller, as Crean has so often demanded. Zeller finished 8-for-14 from the field and helped himself with eight rebounds, including four on offense. He took advantage of Cooley's foul trouble — the 6-foot-9, 248-pounder played 21 minutes before fouling out — and abused the other players the Irish tried to put on him. He also finished with two blocks and two assists.

"We gotta play through Cody all the time," Hulls said. "He can do so many different things. You throw it in, he can either score or he can pass. We just gotta cut off him and find open spots. He's unselfish so he'll find the open man. It's very crucial that we do it every game."

Head coach Tom Crean watches Indiana Hoosiers guard Jordan Hulls.

Said Notre Dame coach Mike Brey: "I don't think we did a very good job of defending him early. We got caught behind him deep. I thought he got a lot of offensive boards to get himself started. I think the first 10 minutes we were pretty good, and we had him pushed out. He had to shoot over us, but he had some putbacks to get himself going. Second half, we played way too deep behind him. He's really a talented kid, and he's got great footwork and can spin off you. Certainly, we could not defend him."

The Hoosiers finished with 36 points in the paint and won the rebounding battle, 40-28. Sophomore guard Victor Oladipo had 16 points on 6-of-7 shooting. Hulls had 12, and Watford scored 10

despite shooting 2-for-9 from the field.

After Abell's tip-in at the first-half buzzer, the Hoosiers went on a 9-3 run in the second half to take a 12-point lead with 14:08 to go. The Irish closed to within six, but the Hoosiers kept them from getting closer and emerged from the teeth of their non-conference schedule unbeaten.

Indiana Hoosiers guard Remy Abell (23) celebrates his last second put back to end the half in game two of the Close the Gap Crossroads Classic in Indianapolis.

NOTRE DAME 58

	Min	3PFG	AFG	FT	O-R	A	PF	Pts
Martin, f	36	0- 1	1- 4	4- 8	0- 7	2	2	6
Cooley, f	21	0- 0	4- 5	4- 5	2- 5	0	5	12
Atkins, g	39	0- 0	5-12	5- 6	1- 2	2	1	15
Drgcevich, g	34	3- 5	3- 6	0- 0	1- 2	0	2	9
Grant, g	36	1- 4	2-10	9-10	0- 4	4	3	14
Cnnaughtn	22	0- 1	1- 3	0- 1	2- 4	1	4	2
Knight	5	0- 0	0- 1	0- 2	0- 0	0	1	0
Brooks	4	0- 0	0- 1	0- 0	0- 0	0	0	0
Broghammer	3	0- 0	0- 0	0- 0	0- 0	0	2	0
team					1- 4			
Totals		4-11	16-42	22-32	7-28	9	20	58
Shooting		.364	.381	.688				

INDIANA 69

	Min	3PFG	AFG	FT	O-R	A	PF	Pts
Watford, f	32	0- 0	2- 9	6- 6	0- 2	1	2	10
Zeller, f	27	0- 0	8-14	5- 6	4- 8	2	4	21
Hulls, g	30	2- 2	4- 9	2- 2	1- 2	3	3	12
Oladipo, g	24	1- 2	6- 7	3- 5	1- 3	1	4	16
Jones, g	33	0- 1	1- 5	2- 3	1- 6	1	4	4
Sheehey	25	0- 0	1- 7	0- 0	4- 9	1	1	2
Moore	1	0- 0	0- 0	0- 0	0- 0	0	0	0
Abell	7	0- 0	1- 2	0- 0	1- 2	0	3	2
Pritchard	10	0- 0	0- 0	0- 0	0- 1	0	4	0
Elston	11	0- 2	1- 4	0- 0	0- 0	0	0	2
team					4- 7			
Totals		3- 7	24-57	18-22	16-40	9	25	69
Shooting		.429	.421	.818				

Notre Dame (7-5)	20	38—58
Indiana (10-0)	26	43—69

Blocks: Notre Dame 5 (Martin 3, Cooley, Knight), Indiana 2 (Zeller 2). **Turnovers:** Notre Dame 12 (Martin 3, Dragicevich 3, Atkins 2,Cooley 2, Connaughton, Brooks), Indiana 11 (Hulls 3, Sheehey 3, Jones 2, Elston 2, Zeller). **Steals:** Notre Dame 6 (Atkins 3, Grant, Cooley, Connaughton), Indiana 4 (Hulls, Watford, Zeller, Elston). **Officials:** Ed Hightower, Jim Burr, Earl Walton. **A:** 19,064.

Head coach Tom Crean during the Indiana Notre Dame men's basketball game.

Verdell Jones III enters the floor at the start of the Indiana Notre Dame men's basketball game.

Indiana Hoosiers forward Cody Zeller (40) shoots over Ohio State Buckeyes forward Jared Sullinger (0) during the Indiana Ohio State men's basketball game at Assembly Hall in Bloomington, Ind., Saturday, Dec. 31, 2011. Indiana won 74-70.

Hoosiers Do It Again

IU upsets No. 2 Ohio State, 74-70

By Dustin Dopirak

This time there were no students — or at least not enough of a consolidated group of them among the sold-out New Year's Eve Assembly Hall crowd — to storm the floor, so Indiana coach Tom Crean had most of it to himself.

He rushed to one side of the floor and gestured to the roaring crowd in the East stands by raising his arms up from under him like he was bowling with both hands. He then turned to the West stands and did the same.

The crowd had given him exactly what he'd asked for — an atmosphere that nearly matched the one that was in Assembly Hall on Dec. 10 when the Hoosiers upset then-No. 1 Kentucky, despite the fact that Saturday's game came during the semester break. His team paid them back with a performance that was on that level and perhaps even more important to the journey for this revived Indiana program.

Thanks to an inspired defensive performance late in the game that included four forced turnovers and a contested — and missed — 3-pointer in the last 1:24, the No. 13 Hoosiers prevailed over No. 2 Ohio State, 74-70, in front of 17,427 in a game that featured nine ties and 11 lead changes. The Hoosiers improved to 13-1 and became the first Indiana team in school history to defeat both the No. 1 and No. 2 team in the same season.

They'd only played both once before, losing to No. 1 Kentucky but beating No. 2 Notre Dame in December of 1977.

"It just signifies where this program's going," said junior forward Christian Watford, who hit two free throws to seal the victory. "We've been through a lot the last couple of years. We've endured the fight and we've been fighting ever since. It's a great accomplishment to beat 1 and 2, but we feel like there's more out there for us."

Saturday's win may indicate perhaps even more than the win over Kentucky that the Hoosiers (13-1 overall, 1-1 in the Big Ten) can be legitimate Big Ten contenders, something that was in question after Wednesday's 80-65 loss at Michigan State. Since Crean was hired in 2008 amid the Kelvin Sampson recruiting sanctions and subsequent roster purge, the Buckeyes have been a team, perhaps more than any other in the conference, that had a talent level that Indiana couldn't hope to touch. The Hoosiers had lost six straight to the Buckeyes since 2008. All were by double-digits, and they came by an average of 19.3 points.

"In the past couple of years, we've gone through every thing you can imagine," sophomore guard Victor Oladipo said. "All that stuff we go through, we can't come out here and get punked. We just went toe-to-toe with them. They've been punking us for the past couple of years. This year, we had to go toe-to-toe with them, and we came out with a victory."

After a largely miserable offensive night at Michigan State, the Hoosiers had five scorers in double figures on Saturday, despite playing without injured sophomore swingman Will Sheehey. Junior guard Jordan Hulls led the way with 17 points, hitting four 3-pointers. Oladipo had 15 to go with six rebounds, including a fastbreak-layup that gave the Hoosiers the lead for good. Freshman forward Cody Zeller had 14 points despite fouling out in just 21 minutes of play. Jones also scored 14 and Watford added 10.

Ohio State (13-2, 1-1) had three scorers in double figures. Sophomore point guard Aaron Craft had 16 to go with four assists. Sophomore forward Jared Sullinger had 15 points and nine rebounds and sophomore guard Lenzelle Smith had 12, but the Buckeyes were stifled by foul trouble for most of the evening. Sullinger, senior guard William Buford and sophomore forward DeShaun Thomas all finished with four fouls. Each had picked up at least three by the 12:22 mark of the second half and each had to sit out at least the last five minutes of the first half with two fouls.

"It made them use their bench," Jones said. "A lot of the film we watched, they went six deep, maybe seven. Today they used a lot of guys that usually don't get much playing time. Playing in an atmosphere like this is different."

That allowed the Hoosiers to quickly erase Ohio State's 10-point first half lead and match them possession for possession in the second half. No team led by more than four points in the entire period.

The Buckeyes took a 70-69 lead on a jumper by Thomas with 1:53 to go, but the Buckeyes gave it away on the next two possessions. On the second, Hulls deflected a pass that went off junior forward Derek Elston into the hands of Jones. Jones found Oladipo streaking down the other end of the floor for a layup that made it 71-70 with 36 seconds to go.

"Defense was what really got us the lead in the first place when we had it," Hulls said. "That's what kept us in the game. We were just staying active. (Jones) did a great job there at the end of forcing a turnover, making him throw a bad pass and we got a deflection."

On the ensuring possession, Craft forced his way close to the paint and tried to force a bounce pass between defenders to freshman swingman Sam Thompson, but Thompson fumbled it away, forcing the Buckeyes to foul with 15 seconds. left.

The Hoosiers put Hulls on the line, and he surprisingly made just one of two. But on the next possession, Buford took an off balance 3-pointer with six seconds left and missed. Watford grabbed the rebound and made two free throws with 2.9 seconds left. Oladipo then leaped up to steal deep inbound pass to seal a victory with a magnitude that seemed unthinkable for this group before this season, but that this team has already accomplished twice.

"The first two years make you really take a step back and just picture what it was two years ago, and to be 13-1, it's an unbelievable feeling," Elston said. "... There's only better things to come."

(Right) Indiana Hoosiers forward Derek Elston (32) commits a foul.

(Below, right) Ohio State Buckeyes forward Jared Sullinger (0) celebrates making the bucket and getting Indiana Hoosiers forward Cody Zeller (40) his fifth foul.

(Below) Indiana Hoosiers guard Remy Abell (23).

OHIO STATE 70

	Min	3PFG	AFG	FT	O-R	A	PF	Pts
Sullinger, f	29	0- 0	3- 5	9-13	0- 9	1	4	15
Thomas, f	21	0- 1	2- 6	1- 2	2- 3	0	4	5
Craft, g	38	1- 1	6-10	3- 4	1- 5	4	2	16
Smith, g	30	2- 3	4- 8	2- 2	2- 6	3	1	12
Buford, g	26	0- 2	3- 7	2- 2	0- 4	3	4	8
Sibert	7	0- 3	0- 3	0- 0	0- 1	0	0	0
Scott	2	0- 0	0- 0	0- 0	0- 0	0	0	0
Thompson	17	0- 1	3- 6	0- 0	1- 1	0	1	6
Weatherspn	4	0- 0	0- 0	0- 0	0- 0	0	0	0
Willaims	7	0- 0	2- 2	0- 1	2- 2	0	2	4
Ravenel	19	0- 0	1- 2	2- 2	0- 3	0	4	4
team					1- 1			
Totals		3-11	24-49	19-26	9-35	11	22	70
Shooting		.273	.490	.731				

INDIANA 74

	Min	3PFG	AFG	FT	O-R	A	PF	Pts
Watford, f	35	0- 2	3-10	4- 6	1- 6	2	2	10
Zeller, f	21	0- 0	5- 9	4- 7	3- 4	0	5	14
Hulls, g	31	4- 5	6- 9	1- 2	0- 2	2	2	17
Oladipo, g	35	1- 4	7-13	0- 0	1- 6	1	1	15
Jones, g	34	0- 2	4-11	6- 6	1- 3	1	2	14
Etherington	2	0- 0	0- 0	0- 0	0- 0	0	1	0
Abell	4	0- 0	0- 1	0- 0	0- 0	0	0	0
Pritchard	9	0- 0	0- 0	0- 0	0- 0	0	0	0
Roth	13	0- 0	0- 0	0- 0	0- 1	0	0	0
Elston	16	0- 0	2- 6	0- 1	2- 4	0	3	4
team					1- 2			
Totals		5-13	27-59	15-22	9-28	6	20	74
Shooting		.385	.458	.682				

Ohio State (13-1)	32	38—70	
Indiana (13-1)	33	41—74	

Blocks: Ohio State 5 (Ravenel 3, Sullinger, Thompson), Indiana 4 (Watford, Hulls, Oladipo, Elston). **Turnovers:** Ohio State 17 (Craft 6, Sullinger 3, Buford 2, Ravenel 2, Thomas, Smith, Sbert, Scott), Indiana 12 (Jones 6, Watford, Zeller, Huls, Oladipo, Pritchard, team). **Steals:** Ohio State 6 (Sullinger 2, Craft 2, Smith, Buford), Indiana 7 (Oladipo 3, Jones 2, Watford, Elston). **Officials:** Terry Wymer, Scott Thornley, Mike Sanzere. **A:** 17,472.

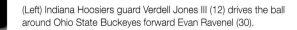
(Left) Indiana Hoosiers guard Verdell Jones III (12) drives the ball around Ohio State Buckeyes forward Evan Ravenel (30).

(Above) Indiana Hoosiers forward Tom Pritchard (25) goes up to defend the basket.

(Above) Indiana Hoosiers guard Victor Oladipo (4) defends the inbound bass of Ohio State Buckeyes guard William Buford (44).

Head coach Tom Crean celebrates with the crowd at mid-court after the Indiana Ohio State game.

27

Michigan Wolverines guard Trey Burke (3) shoots over
Indiana Hoosiers forward Tom Pritchard (25) during the
Indiana Michigan men's basketball game at Assembly Hall in
Bloomington, Ind., Thursday, Jan. 5, 2012.

Hoosiers Hold Off Michigan

No. 12 Indiana survives rally by 16th- ranked Wolverines, 73-71

By Dustin Dopirak

The reason Indiana coach Tom Crean says he doesn't want his team to ever feel like it can take a breath and exhale is games like this one.

No. 12 Indiana led No. 16 Michigan by as many as 15 points in the first half of Thursday night's game and by double digits at points throughout the second half. But the Hoosiers learned that even at home they are not invincible against forces like 3-pointers. They never trailed, but they never got to exhale until Michigan senior swingman Zack Novak's desperation heave bounced off the right side of the backboard.

Still, the Hoosiers claimed their third victory over a ranked opponent in their revival season, downing the Wolverines 73-71 in front of 16,020 at Assembly Hall on Thursday night thanks to dominant performances by forwards Christian Watford and Cody Zeller and an icy, last-minute, late-in-the-shot-clock jumper by senior guard Verdell Jones III.

It's the first time since the 2005-06 season that the Hoosiers have defeated at least three ranked opponents in one season, and it's the first time since the 2007-08 campaign that they've started the season 14-1.

"This is a big time win for us," Crean said. "This is a big-time win over a big-time team and we gritted it out."

Said Jones: "I just think it's a testament to our off-season work. Being able to fight through stuff when it gets tough. I think that's what we did today. They made a lot of runs, but we just kept fighting tooth and nail to get back in it. I thought they made some big plays at the end, but we stayed focused and stayed hungry."

Michigan had four scorers in double-figures and hit 10 of its 24 3-pointers, while the Hoosiers had just two scorers in double-figures and hit 10 of its 24 3-pointers, while the Hoosiers had just two scorers in double figures for the first time all season. However, Watford's 25 points and Zeller's 18 were enough to carry them, and Watford was especially dominant. He was 8-for-11 from the field, 3-for-4 from beyond the arc, and also had seven rebounds and tied his career-high with four assists.

"I got to the free throw line tonight," Watford said. "That helped me a lot in the second half. In the first half, I just got a couple of layups, got a couple early shots to fall. They don't have a lot of length and stuff like that, so I got some good looks."

The Hoosiers took control of the game in the first half thanks in large part to the defense of Jones, sophomore guard Victor Ola-dipo and the others who held star Michigan guards Trey Burke and Tim Hardaway Jr., to eight points and a combined 3-for-15 shooting in the first half. Indiana opened the game on a 17-6 run and took a lead as big as 33-18.

Jones was particularly effective on Burke, widely regarded to be Zeller's top competition for Big Ten Freshman of the Year honors. Jones stayed on his hip and harassed him to a 4-for-15 performance.

"It's different being taller and guarding a quick guy like that," Jones said. "I watched a lot of film on him. When they put length on him, he struggles a little bit, and my teammates put great help-side defense on him."

However, Michigan came back using the method teams coached by John Beilein usually do — the 3-pointer. The Wolverines hit three of them in a span of 1:16 at the end of the first half to cut Indiana's lead to five points. The Hoosiers went into the break with a 39-32 advantage, but outscored Michigan 14-6 in the last 5:08. Novak hit a 3-pointer to start the second half, and that kept the lane open for the early part of the half, and the Wolverines were able to attack a spread-out Indiana defense, which was hurt by foul trouble to Oladipo. They opened the half on a 14-7 run to tie the game at 46 with 14:57 left.

"Any time a team can shoot like that, they always have a chance to be in it or win the game," Jones said. "The 3-ball is a special weapon. They hit a lot of good shots."

The Hoosiers started hitting some of their own midway through the second half, going on 12-4 run that gave them a 65-55 advantage on a high-flying dunk by Oladipo. Just as quickly, however, Michigan answered with a 13-3 run to tie it at 68 with 3:02 to go on a dunk by Hardaway.

But Indiana took the lead on two free throws by Jones, then made three straight critical stops as Michigan finally went cold from the 3-point arc. The Hoosiers got the ball with 1:01 left in the game and needed to milk clock, but also needed to hit a shot to put it away, and that was where Jones came in.

The Hoosiers called timeout with 39 seconds to go and Oladipo tried to make a play but couldn't find any space. Jones got the ball with about six seconds to go on the shot clock needing to make something happen fast. The mid-range ace and 1,000-point scorer took two dribbles to his left and nailed one from about 17 feet to make it 72-68.

"Oh, my goodness that was huge," Crean said. "To knock that down, like that, that's him. Going left, pull-up jumper. It was basically broken at that point. It was make a play."

That didn't put it away quite yet. Novak turned the ball over on the other end, but Jones missed the front end of a 1-and-1 that would've sealed it. Michigan made one more play with four seconds to go when senior guard Stu Douglass drilled a 3-pointer to make it 72-71 to maintain the drama.

Watford was fouled on the inbound and made just one of two free throws to make it 73-71, giving Michigan a shot at a miracle, but Novak missed and allowed IU to breathe and escape.

"This team gritted it out again," Crean said. "They toughed it out again."

(Below) Indiana Hoosiers guard Jordan Hulls (1) defends Michigan Wolverines guard Trey Burke (3).

MICHIGAN 71

	Min	3PFG	AFG	FT	O- R	A	PF	Pts
Smotrycz, f	25	2- 3	3- 6	0- 0	1- 2	1	4	8
Morgan, f	34	0- 0	6- 7	0- 0	2- 9	0	2	12
Novak, g	24	2- 3	3- 5	0- 0	0- 4	0	3	8
Burke, g	38	2- 5	4-15	0- 3	3- 7	8	1	10
Hardaway, g	37	0- 7	7-19	5- 6	1- 4	2	2	19
Douglass	30	3- 5	3- 5	2- 2	0- 2	2	5	11
Vogrich	5	0- 0	0- 0	0- 0	0- 0	0	0	0
McLimans	7	1- 1	1- 1	1- 0	0- 0	0	0	3
team					2- 2			
Totals		10-24	27-58	7-11	9-30	13	17	71
Shooting		.417	.466	.636				

INDIANA 73

	Min	3PFG	AFG	FT	O- R	A	PF	Pts
Watford, f	33	3- 4	8-11	6- 8	0- 7	4	2	25
Zeller, f	32	0- 0	8-10	2- 2	2- 4	0	2	18
Hulls, g	29	1- 1	1- 4	0- 0	0- 2	2	3	3
Oladipo, g	24	0- 3	2-10	1- 2	0- 4	2	4	5
Jones, g	34	0- 0	3- 6	2- 2	6- 3	8		8
Etherington	1	0- 0	0- 0	0- 0	1- 0	0	0	0
Abell	6	1- 1	1- 1	3- 0	0- 1	1	0	3
Pritchard	12	0- 0	0- 0	0- 1	2- 2	3	0	1
Roth	14	1- 1	1- 2	2- 0	0- 1	1	0	5
Elston	15	1- 1	2- 3	0- 0	0- 4	0	0	5
team					2- 3			
Totals		7-11	27-49	12-19	7-31	15	15	73
Shooting		.636	.551	.632				

Indiana Hoosiers guard Verdell Jones III (12) is introduced during the Indiana Michigan men's basketball game at Assembly Hall in Bloomington, Ind., Thursday, Jan. 5, 2012.

Michigan (12-3)	32	39—71
Indiana (14-1)	39	34—73

Blocks: Michigan 1 (Douglass), Indiana 6 (Zeller 2, Oladipo 2, Pritchard, Elston. **Turnovers:** Michigan 12 (Burke 4, Hardawy 3, Smotrycz 2, Novak, Douglass, Vogrich), Indiana 15 (Jones 4, Watford, Zeller 3, Hulls 2, Oladipo 2, Abell). **Steals:** Michigan 8 (Hardaway 3, Smotrycz, Morgan, Novak, Burke, Douglass), Indiana 5 (Oladipo 2, Hulls, Jones, Roth). **Officials:** Jim Burr, Bo Boroski, Mark Whitehead. A: 16,020.

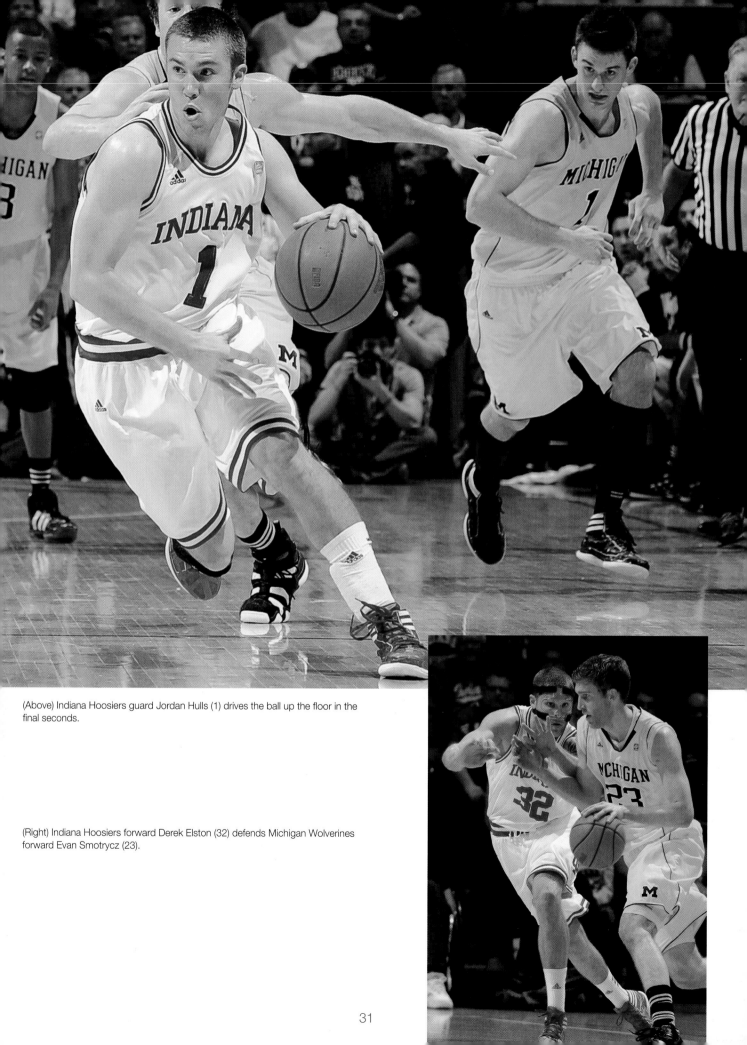

(Above) Indiana Hoosiers guard Jordan Hulls (1) drives the ball up the floor in the final seconds.

(Right) Indiana Hoosiers forward Derek Elston (32) defends Michigan Wolverines forward Evan Smotrycz (23).

Indiana Hoosiers forward Cody Zeller (40) pump fakes Nebraska Cornhuskers guard Bo Spencer (23) and Nebraska Cornhuskers guard Brandon Richardson (3) during the Indiana Nebraska men's basketball game at the Bob Devaney Arena in Lincoln, Neb.

Hoosiers in Free Fall

Lowly Nebraska hands Indiana 3rd straight Big Ten loss, 70-69

By Dustin Dopirak

When Jordan Hulls' desperation heave off his own miss clanked off the backboard and the rim, the Indiana Hoosiers found out what it was like to have the court stormed on them.

Unlike the Kentucky players who found themselves toppled during the mayhem at Assembly Hall on Dec. 10, the Hoosiers had plenty of room Wednesday night to trudge off the Devaney Center floor unmolested with heads hanging and despondent facial expressions after the 70-69 loss. Nebraska's court-storming barely filled the large block "N" at center court, let alone the entire floor like Hoosier fans did on a night that suddenly seems like a distant memory.

Despite building a 13-point second-half lead, the No. 11 Hoosiers never put away Nebraska, and the underdog Cornhuskers made sure they suffered the consequences of that failure. The normally automatic Hulls missed a critical front end of a set of 1-and-1 free throws with 19 seconds to go. Nebraska center Jorge Brian Diaz made two foul shots to give the Huskers a one-point lead with 11 seconds left, and Hulls missed on a layup and a 3-pointer on the game's final possession to give Big Ten newcomer Nebraska the win in front of 8,613.

And after a thrilling 15-1 start, Indiana finds itself trying to avoid panic mode and a free fall that would derail an extremely promising season.

The Hoosiers (15-4 overall, 3-4 in the Big Ten) have lost three straight since cracking the Top 10 in both the Associated Press and ESPN/USA Today polls, including two they were favored to win. The Cornhuskers (10-8, 2-5) had won just one conference game before Wednesday, and that came against a Penn State team that is also largely expected to finish near the bottom of the conference.

Afterward, Indiana coach Tom Crean and his players seemed to be very much in damage control mode. They strained to keep their heads up in post-game interviews, crediting Nebraska and saying they actually believed Wednesday night's game to be an improvement over their previous two losses.

"This league has 12 teams that can play with anybody," Crean said. "We're one of them, as is Nebraska.... You can't get too concerned with records with anybody in this league right now. We certainly never played Nebraska like they'd won one game. We

knew how good they were. Our guys had great edge tonight. They had excellent energy. We did so many good things."

Despite the outcome, they actually did, and in certain ways the box score doesn't seem to add up to an Indiana loss. The Hoosiers shot 51.0 percent from the field (26-for-51), while holding Nebraska to 37.7 percent (23-for-61). They won the rebounding battle 34-32. They moved the ball well for the most part and had at least a hand in causing the Cornhuskers to take 30 of their 61 shots from beyond the 3-point arc. Freshman forward Cody Zeller had yet another efficient performance with 18 points, seven rebounds and two assists, and Hulls chipped in with 12.

But there were critical flaws that burned them in their last two losses that came back to haunt them again. They committed 15 turnovers in the game, including 10 in the second half that turned into 10 Nebraska points, which were a big part of the reason the Huskers stayed in the game.

"We've got to take care of the ball better," Crean said. "I think we're going to go back and look at the film, and we're going to look at the turnovers in the second half and just see how excruciatingly painful those were for us, because those turned into more easy baskets for Nebraska.... I think it was just our strength with the ball and some decision making."

Nebraska, meanwhile, just kept shooting until shots started falling. They made just six of their first 22 3-point attempts but knocked down four of their last eight. Star senior guard Bo Spencer shot through slumps and finished with 23 points on 8-for-19 shooting. Senior guard Toney McCray scored 11. Diaz and senior guard Dylan Talley scored 10 each.

"We ran stuff, and we executed it," Nebraska coach Doc Sadler said. "We were calling a play every time, and the guys executed it. We missed some, but I really thought ... for the most part, we took good shots."

And even though the Huskers lost the overall rebound battle, they won a critical segment. Indiana grabbed just five offensive rebounds and finished with two second-chance points, while Nebraska got 10 of each, allowing the Huskers to keep shooting.

The Hoosiers were ahead 63-52 with 6:38 to play when Nebraska's shots started going down in a hurry. McCray and Spencer hit 3-pointers during an 8-0 run that made it 63-60 with 4:28 to go, and from there the Huskers kept chipping away until the Hoosiers were clinging to a one-point lead with 38 seconds to go.

Hulls drew a foul and made two free throws with 35 seconds to go before Talley grabbed an offensive rebound and a putback to make it 69-68 with 23.8 seconds left.

And on the following possession Hulls, who earlier this year snapped a Big Ten record streak of 58 consecutive free throws, missed the crucial front end of the 1-and-1.

"He's a human being," Crean said. "Nobody's more disappointed than he is. But you know what? We wouldn't trade having him at the line again. ... He's been phenomenal at the line."

Diaz got position on the low block on the next possession before drawing the foul from Will Sheehey and draining both free throws. The Hoosiers didn't call a timeout on the inbound play even though they had one remaining, and Hulls drove the length of the court. He arguably should've pulled up before going for the layup he missed. The ball was kicked out to the 3-point line, where Hulls grabbed it and threw up an off-balanced prayer that went unanswered, allowing the Hoosiers' slide to continue into Sunday's home game against Penn State.

"We just gotta go back to the drawing board," sophomore guard Victor Oladipo said. "Compete in practice and all of those kind of things and make sure these losses don't pile up."

And ignore the fact that they're already starting to.

"We just got a group of guys that have that edge, that have a desire," Crean said. "We've got to make sure we refocus them, that we re-energize them, and we do not let them get discouraged. We make sure we understand disappointment is inevitable in life, but discouragement is our choice and we choose not to have it."

Nebraska Cornhuskers guard Dylan Talley (24) fouls Indiana Hoosiers forward Cody Zeller (40) as Nebraska Cornhuskers center Jorge Brian Diaz (21) helps defend.

Indiana Hoosiers guard Verdell Jones III (12) loses control of the ball as Nebraska Cornhuskers guard Bo Spencer (23) defends.

INDIANA 69

	Min	3PFG	AFG	FT	O- R	A	PF	Pts
Watford, f	34	1- 2	3- 8	1- 2	2-10	2	1	8
Zeller, f	27	0- 0	7-12	4- 5	2- 7	2	3	18
Hulls, g	35	2- 6	3- 8	4- 5	0- 4	2	1	12
Oladipo, g	25	1- 3	2- 4	0- 0	0- 3	4	1	5
Jones, g	27	0- 0	2- 4	0- 1	1- 6	5	3	4
Sheehey	17	1- 2	3- 6	0- 0	0- 2	1	1	7
Pritchard	13	0- 0	2- 3	0- 0	0- 1	0	2	4
Roth	16	3- 5	3- 5	0- 0	0- 0	1	0	9
Elston	6	0- 0	1- 10	0- 0	0- 0	0	2	2
team					0- 1			
Totals		8-18	26-51	9-13	5-34	17	12	69
Shooting		.444	.510	.692				

NEBRASKA 70

	Min	3PFG	AFG	FT	O- R	A	PF	Pts
Ubel, f	21	0- 1	1- 4	0- 0	0- 4	0	2	2
McCray, g	33	3- 6	4- 9	0- 0	1- 3	3	2	11
Richardson, g	30	1- 3	1- 5	6- 8	0- 4	5	2	9
Spencer, g	34	4-12	8-19	3- 4	0- 1	3	3	23
Walker, g	28	1- 3	2- 4	0- 0	0- 4	0	1	5
Diaz	26	0- 0	3- 9	4- 5	4- 4	1	1	10
Talley	28	1- 5	4-11	1- 2	4- 9	3	4	10
team					1- 3			
Totals		10-30	23-61	14-19	10-32	15	15	70
Shooting		.333	.377	.737				

Indiana (15-4)		41	28—69
Nebraska (9-9)		34	36—70

Blocks: Indiana 2 (Sheehey, Pritchard), Nebraska 3 (Talley 2, Diaz). **Turnovers:** Indiana 15 (Watford 4, Oladipo 3, Zeller 2, Sheehey 2, Hulls, Jones, Roth, team), Nebraska 10 (Spencer 4, Diaz 2, Ubel, McCray, Walker, team). **Steals:** Indiana 3 (Oladipo 2, Sheehey), Nebraska 8 (Richardson 3, McCray 2, Talley 2, Diaz). **Technicals:** Pritchard. **Officials:** Mike Kitts, Mike Sanzere, Gerald Williams. **A:** 8,613.

Head coach Tom Crean points at the clock as the Hoosiers head to halftime.

Nebraska fans streak onto the floor as Indiana Hoosiers forward Christian Watford (2) and Indiana Hoosiers guard/forward Will Sheehey (10) show their dejection after the game.

Indiana Hoosiers guard/forward Will Sheehey (10) passes as Iowa Hawkeyes guard Matt Gatens (5) defends during the Indiana Iowa men's basketball game at Assembly Hall in Bloomington, Ind., Sunday, Jan. 29, 2012.

Hoosiers slam Hawkeyes

Indiana's offensive explosion too much for Iowa, 103-89

By Dustin Dopirak

To an Indiana team that likes its tempo as fast as anyone in the Big Ten, Thursday's game at Wisconsin had to feel like spending a day in a straitjacket.

Playing against Iowa Sunday was pretty much the exact opposite. Just like the No. 16 Hoosiers, the Hawkeyes like their track meets, and Iowa played into the hands of an Indiana team that was thrilled with the opportunity to revel in freedom of motion. Indiana didn't play great defense — especially in the second half, when they allowed the Hawkeyes to shoot 79.2 percent from the field — but it didn't much matter. The Hoosiers outran Iowa 103-89 in front of 17,243 at Assembly Hall, scoring more points in the first half (54) than they did all game in Thursday's 57-50 loss to the Badgers.

The Hoosiers (17-5 overall, 5-5 in the Big Ten) were both faster and more physical than the Hawkeyes (11-11, 3-6). The 103 points was the most scored by any team in a Big Ten game this season, and it was the most the Hoosiers have scored in a conference game since March 12, 1995, when they beat Iowa 110-79. But unlike the last two years when the Hoosiers were handled in four games with the Hawkeyes, Indiana dominated the paint. The Hoosiers won the rebounding battle 37-22, grabbed 20 offensive rebounds that they converted into 23 second-chance points and scored a stunning 58 points in the paint, making for a game that was never within single digits in the second half even as Iowa was shooting 19-for-24.

"To have said what was said about us and what these guys have done to us in the past and to come out and do that and to get to the point where we were putting in (Raphael Smith) and (Taylor Wayer) and (Kory Barnett) and (Jeff Howard) in a Big Ten game, that's huge for us," junior forward Derek Elston said. "... Everybody came out with that toughness that we needed, and we just kind of ran with it. Once we got in a flow, it was hard to stop us." The Hawkeyes had no answer whatsoever for Indiana freshman forward Cody Zeller, who scored a career-high 26 points on an incredible 11-for-12 shooting performance. The 6-foot-11, 230-pounder admitted it was one of his easiest nights since the beginning of Big Ten play. Eight of his 11 field goals came on dunks, in large part because his teammates found him for drop-offs.

"I had a pretty easy job," Zeller said. "Just catch it and dunk it. Our guards did a really nice job of finding me in the alley a couple of times. Verdell (Jones) did a really nice job of finding me."

Jones had arguably his best game of the season. The oft-criticized senior guard scored 14 points and finished with nine assists to just

three turnovers, carving up Iowa with dribble penetration against both man-to-man and zone defenses, forcing them to collapse and leaving Zeller and others open near the basket.

"Verdell's making a lot better decisions," Elston said. "I can definitely tell he's not rushing it anymore. When he gets into the huddles after timeouts, he kind of is letting everybody know what he's going to be doing and where everybody should be at that time. Verdell's decision-making these past couple of days, even in practice, has just been phenomenal. He's kind of just been the team leader so far. He's been the floor general for us, and it really showed tonight."

With Jones pushing the offense into high-gear, it didn't much matter that the Hoosiers didn't get much from beyond the 3-point arc, hitting on just four of 16 attempts. Junior point guard Jordan Hulls played just 18 minutes and missed his only 3-point attempt, and senior guard Matt Roth was 0-for-2 from 3-point land in just four minutes after missing the last two days of practice with an illness.

The Hoosiers still shot 55.2 percent from the field and put six players in double figures for the first time since their 107-50 win over Howard on Dec. 19. Junior forward Christian Watford had 15 points and seven rebounds. Sophomore guard Victor Oladipo broke out of his slump with 12 points, six rebounds and three assists. Elston hit two 3-pointers and finished with 11 points, while sophomore swingman Will Sheehey — who got his first start of the season in place of Oladipo — had 10 points, four rebounds and two assists. The Hoosiers finished with 20 assists to just 13 turnovers.

"The bottom line," Indiana coach Tom Crean said, "was that the ball moved."

The ball moved for Iowa as well, and there will be some ugly defensive numbers for the Hoosiers to eventually digest. Iowa shot 63 percent from the field (34-for-54), the highest mark of any Indiana opponent this season. Freshman guard Josh Oglesby scored 24 points thanks to six 3-pointers. Senior guard Matt Gatens scored 20 points, and sophomore guard Roy Devyn Marble had 13.

But for the most part, the Hoosiers' defensive woes were never a reason for concern. They went on a 22-6 run at the end of the first half to take a 54-37 lead at the half, holding the Hawkeyes without a field goal in the last 4:07. Iowa was never again closer than 12 points, and the Hoosiers avenged four straight losses at the Hawkeyes' hands.

Indiana Hoosiers forward Tom Pritchard (25) dunks the put back rebound over Iowa Hawkeyes center Gabriel Olaseni (0) during the Indiana Iowa men's basketball game at Assembly Hall in Bloomington, Ind., Sunday, Jan. 29, 2012. Indiana won 103-89.

IOWA 89

	Min	3PFG	AFG	FT	O- R	A	PF	Pts
McCabe, f	21	0- 0	1- 3	1- 1	1- 2	0	3	3
White, f	23	1- 2	4- 9	0- 1	0- 1	1	5	9
Marble, g	33	0- 1	6- 9	1- 2	1- 3	5	1	13
Gatens, g	35	1- 4	9-13	1- 1	1- 2	0	2	20
Crtwright, g	25	0- 0	2- 2	4- 6	0- 2	8	3	8
Olaseni	9	0- 0	0- 1	2- 4	0- 1	0	1	2
Basabe	13	0- 0	2- 3	2- 4	2- 3	0	4	6
Oglesby	20	6- 8	8-12	2- 2	0- 1	1	1	24
McCarty	1	0- 0	0- 0	0- 0	0- 0	0	0	0
Brommer	2	0- 0	0- 0	0- 0	0- 0	0	0	0
May	5	0- 0	0- 0	0- 0	1- 1	0	0	0
Stubbs	3	0- 0	1- 1	0- 0	0- 0	1	0	2
Stokes	1	0- 0	0- 0	0- 0	0- 0	0	0	0
Archie	9	0- 0	1- 1	0- 0	0- 2	0	3	2
team					1- 4			
Totals		8-15	34-54	13-21	7-22	16	23	89
Shooting		.533	.630	.619				

INDIANA 103

	Min	3PFG	AFG	FT	O- R	A	PF	Pts
Watford, f	27	0- 3	4-10	7- 8	4- 7	0	1	15
Zeller, f	28	0- 0	11-12	4- 6	0- 4	4	3	26
Hulls, g	18	0- 1	3- 4	0- 0	0- 1	2	2	6
Sheehey, g	23	2- 2	2- 5	4- 4	2- 4	2	3	10
Jones, g	31	0- 3	4-10	6- 7	0- 2	9	2	14
Barnett	2	0- 1	1- 2	0- 0	0- 0	0	0	2
Oladipo	22	0- 1	5- 8	2- 2	5- 6	3	1	12
Etherington	4	0- 1	0- 2	0- 0	1- 1	0	1	0
Smith	1	0- 0	0- 0	0- 0	0- 0	0	0	0
Wayer	1	0- 0	0- 0	0- 0	0- 0	0	0	0
Abell	7	0- 0	0- 2	0- 0	1- 2	0	0	0
Howard	1	0- 0	0- 0	0- 0	0- 0	0	0	0
Pritchard	13	0- 0	3- 5	1- 2	3- 4	0	1	7
Roth	4	0- 2	0- 2	0- 0	0- 2	1	0	0
Elston	18	2- 2	4- 5	1- 2	2- 2	0	2	11
team					2- 2			
Totals		4-16	37-67	25-31	20-37	20	17	103
Shooting		.250	.552	.806				

Indiana Hoosiers forward Tom Pritchard (25) gets high fives for his play during the Indiana Iowa men's basketball game at Assembly Hall in Bloomington, Ind., Sunday, Jan. 29, 2012.

Iowa (11-11)	37	52—	89
Indiana (17-5)	54	49—	103

Blocks: Iowa 6 (Olaseni 2, Basabe 2, McCabe, Marble), Indiana 5 (Elston 2, Zeller, Jones, Oladipo). **Turnovers:** Iowa 17 (Cartwright 6, Gatens 4, White 2, McCabe, Olaseni, Basabe, Oglesby, May), Indiana 13 (Watford 3, Jones 3, Hulls 2, Sheehey 2, Elston 2, Abell). **Steals:** Iowa 6 (Gatens 4, Marble, Cartwright), Indiana 7 (Zeller 3, Watford, Hulls, Oladipo, Pritchard). **Officials:** Ed Hightower, Mike Eades, D.J. Carstensen. **A:** 17,243.

Indiana Hoosiers forward Derek Elston (32) celebrates hitting a 3-pointer.

Iowa Hawkeyes guard Josh Oglesby (2) drives by Indiana Hoosiers guard Jordan Hulls (1).

Indiana Hoosiers forward Derek Elston (32) shoots over Iowa Hawkeyes forward Aaron White (30).

Iowa Hawkeyes guard/forward Roy Devyn Marble (4) tips the pass intended for Indiana Hoosiers forward Christian Watford (2).

Indiana Hoosiers forward Cody Zeller (40) stretches for the rebound during the Indiana Iowa men's basketball game at Assembly Hall in Bloomington, Ind., Sunday, Jan. 29, 2012.

Purdue Boilermakers forward
Robbie Hummel (4) deflects the shot of
Indiana Hoosiers guard Victor Oladipo
(4) during the Indiana Purdue men's
basketball game
in West Lafayette, Ind.,
Saturday, Feb. 4, 2012.

Hoosiers Put Away Boilers, 78-61

Abell's 3, career night from Oladipo lead IU to rare Big Ten road win

By Dustin Dopirak

Robbie Hummel didn't even put his hand up for a close out on Remy Abell until the freshman had already let go of the shot. The heady Purdue senior forward had read enough of the book on the Indiana guard to know that his first instinct when catching the ball beyond the 3-point arc would be to attack the basket off the dribble.

"The scouting report on him is, probably, let him shoot in that situation because he hasn't been in there," Hummel said. "I was kind of playing for the drive."

Instead of flying out with his hands up on the defensive rotation, Hummel sprinted to a spot a few feet from the arc and broke down his feet to be ready for the drive. But Abell pulled up and drilled a shot that stunned the veteran and took the air out of what had been an ear-piercing Mackey Arena in a 78-61 win.

Abell's basket gave the Hoosiers a 70-61 lead with 1:27 to go and essentially assured that this time, they weren't going to blow a late lead on the road, and this time, they were finally going to beat Purdue.

The win snapped a five-game losing streak against their in-state foe that goes back to 2008 and gave their seniors their first victory in the IU-Purdue rivalry. It also snapped a four-game road losing streak for the Hoosiers (18-6 overall, 6-6 in the Big Ten) and gave them just their third Big Ten road win in the Tom Crean era and their first in a building other than Penn State's relatively tame Bryce Jordan Center. This one could be critical in so many ways for post-season positioning in both the Big Ten Tournament and the NCAA Tournament.

"We've been struggling on the road, man," said sophomore guard Victor Oladipo, who led all scorers with a career-high 23 points. "This is a big road win for us. We just gotta continue to keep doing it, continue to play at a high level."

There were times when neither squad was playing at a high level, particularly in a brutal first half in which the two teams combined to shoot a ghastly 19-for-74 (25.7 percent) allowing the Hoosiers to grab 34 rebounds — 0.3 short of their season average — in the first half.

But the Hoosiers' will throughout so impressed Purdue coach Matt Painter that he said it would have been an injustice if the Boilermakers had pulled it out.

"To me it looked like it meant more to them right from the start," Painter said. "You just see guys' facial expressions, you can see guys' body language. I thought they were more engaged. If we could've made that play at the end when we were down four and they ended up losing, it would've been a shame, because they deserved to win the game. They were tougher than us, they were quicker to the basketball."

Three days after coming out flat, coming back then fading late at Michigan, the Hoosiers put forth arguably their best defensive effort of the season, holding the Boilermakers (15-8, 5-5) to 8-for-40 shooting (20 percent) in the first half and 21-for-71 (29.6 percent) for the game and grabbing a season-high 53 rebounds to Purdue's 35.

They were without senior guard Verdell Jones III, who sat out with a bruised shoulder, and got stellar performances from both Oladipo and Abell, who handled the ball more than they had all season and carved up the Purdue defense by slashing to the basket. Oladipo scored his 23 points on 6-for-14 shooting and a 10-for-12 performance behind the line. He hit a 3-pointer to break out of a 3-for-22 slump and he also had eight rebounds, four assists, two blocks against just two turnovers.

"I thought his decision making was really good," Indiana coach Tom Crean said. "He was very good at the ball screen. He was very good at finding people."

Abell had 13 points in a career-high 19 minutes, and that opened things up for freshman forward Cody Zeller, who finished with 16 points and eight rebounds.

But as always seems to happen when they have a lead on the road, the Hoosiers had to fend off a late rally. They led 33-22 at the half and kept it around double-digits for most of the early part of the second half. However, the Boilermakers cut it to four on a putback by freshman guard Lewis Jackson with 3:17 to go and then to four gain with 2:54 left.

However, the Hoosiers got a critical play from sophomore guard Will Sheehey, who swatted an attempted layup by Jackson with 2:18 to go that would've made it 65-63.

"There's watershed moments in a game that you can point to to say that these were crucial parts of the game," Crean said. "That block was one of them. And Remy making the shot was one of them."

Abell's shot opened up thanks to a drive from Oladipo to make the defense collapse. He kicked it back to junior forward Christian Watford, who made the extra pass to find Abell.

"They kicked it over and I was wide open," Abell said. "Somebody stepped up. Christian did a nice job of throwing me the extra pass and I just knocked it down."

Head coach Tom Crean

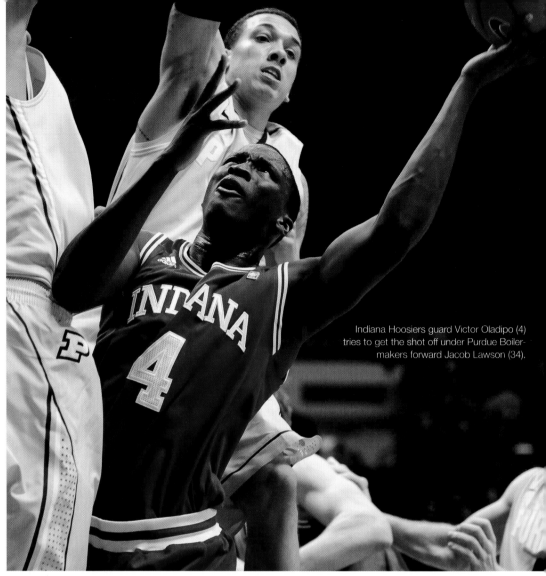

Indiana Hoosiers guard Victor Oladipo (4) tries to get the shot off under Purdue Boiler-makers forward Jacob Lawson (34).

INDIANA 78

	Min	3PFG	AFG	FT	O-	R	A	PF	Pts
Watford, f	28	0-3	0-7	4-4	1-	6	2	1	4
Elston, f	18	0-1	1-6	3-4	1-	6	0	2	5
Zeller, f	32	0-4	7-8	11-3	8-		1	3	16
Hulls, g	34	0-3	4-10	2-2	10	3	2	0	10
Oladipo, g	30	1-1	6-14	10-12	3-	8	4	3	23
Barnett	1	0-0	0-0	0-0	0-	0	0	0	0
Sheehey	22	1-1	3-4	0-0	2-	7	1	1	7
Moore	1	0-0	0-0	0-0	0-	0	0	0	0
Abell	19	1-1	5-6	2-2	1-	4	0	2	13
Pritchard	8	0-0	0-0	0-0	0-	0	0	3	0
Roth	7	0-0	0-1	0-0	0-	2	2	0	0
team					4-	9			
Totals		3-10	23-55	29-35	16-53		10	17	78
Shooting		.300	.418	.829					

PURDUE 61

	Min	3PFG	AFG	FT	O-	R	A	PF	Pts
Johnson, f	30	0-2	2-12	0-0	0-	4	0	3	4
Hummel, f	35	0-2	4-14	8-9	3-10		2	2	16
Carroll, c	9	0-0	0-0	0-0	0-1		1	1	4	0
Jackson, g	30	0-1	1-10	0-0	1-	2	4	1	2
Smith, g	28	2-7	3-9	0-0	1-2		0	4	8
Johnson	9	0-1	0-2	0-0	2-0		1	1	0
Barlow	26	0-2	4-10	4-7	1-	2	0	1	12
Byrd	20	3-5	5-10	2-2	1-	2	0	5	15
Hart	3	0-1	0-1	0-0	0-	0	0	0	0
Lawson	7	0-0	1-2	0-0	2-	2	0	1	2
Marcius	3	0-0	1-1	0-0	0-	3	4	0	3	2
team					2-	5		1	
Totals		5-21	21-71	14-20	15-35		8	26	61
Shooting		.238	.296	.700					

The Hoosier bench celebrates teammate Indiana Hoosiers guard Remy Abell (23) 3-pointer.

Indiana (18-6)	33	45	78
Purdue (15-8)	22	39	61

Blocks: Indiana 7 (Sheehey 3, Oladipo 2, Watford, Zeller), Purdue 8 (Hummel 5, Johnson, Carroll, Byrd). **Turnovers:** Indiana 11 (Hulls 4, Zeller 2, Oladipo 2, Elston, Abell, Roth), Purdue 3 (Johnson, Hummel, Jackson). **Steals:** Indiana 1 (Sheehey), Purdue 7 (Hummel 2, Jackson 2, Carroll, Barlow, Lawson). **Techincals:** Purdue bench. **Officials:** Ted Valentine, Mike Sanzere, Pat Driscoll. **A:** 15,108.

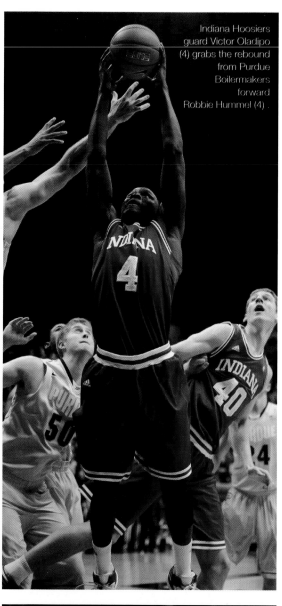

Indiana Hoosiers guard Victor Oladipo (4) grabs the rebound from Purdue Boilermakers forward Robbie Hummel (4) .

Indiana Hoosiers guard Jordan Hulls (1) congratulates teammate Indiana Hoosiers forward Derek Elston (32) on his play.

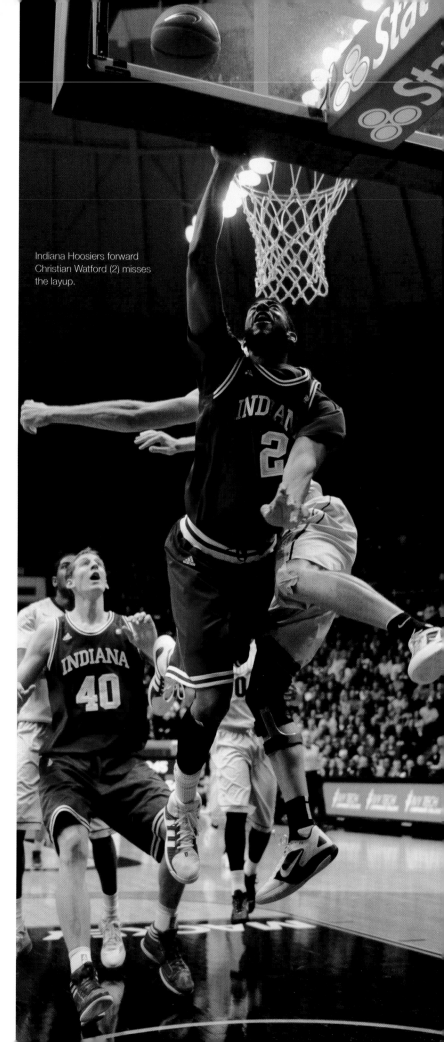

Indiana Hoosiers forward Christian Watford (2) misses the layup.

Indiana Hoosiers forward
Will Sheehey (10) rips down
the rebound as Minnesota
Golden Gophers guard
Austin Hollins (20) defends
during the Indiana Minnesota
basketball game at Williams Arena
in Minneapolis, Minn.,
Sunday, Feb. 26, 2012.
Indiana won 69-50.

Indiana Buries Gophers, 69-50

INDIANA 69
MINNESOTA 50

WILLIAMS ARENA
MINNEAPOLIS, MINNESOTA

Hoosiers shut down Minnesota to claim road win

By Dustin Dopirak

Tom Crean had prepared himself for exactly this sort of occasion. The Indiana coach has long been one to let his team play through tough stretches instead of calling a timeout. That's burned him on several occasions this year in Big Ten road games—most notably during the loss at Nebraska—when teams were able to extend runs with the home crowd behind them, and he vowed not to let that happen again.

But when Minnesota opened Sunday's game with back-to-back 3-pointers, Crean went with his gut and his base philosophy and let his team play.

"One of my notes to myself in big letters is, 'Do not let them get on a run, go timeout early," Crean said. "But I didn't want to do that to my team at 6-0, because they were so ready to play. There was no doubt about it."

This time, he was very much right.

The No. 23 Hoosiers answered with a 9-0 run and never trailed again, pounding Minnesota 69-50 in front of 11,421 at Williams Arena. It was Indiana's first win at "The Barn" since 2008 and just their fourth there since 1993.

The margin of victory was IU's largest in a conference game this season since a 73-54 win against Penn State on Jan. 22 and largest margin in a Big Ten road game since beating Penn State 75-56 on Feb. 11, 2004.

It was a critical win for the Hoosiers (22-7 overall, 9-7 in the Big Ten), who avenged their only loss at Assembly Hall this season, a 77-74 Minnesota victory on Jan. 12. They clinched at least a .500 record in conference play, surpassing their total of eight league wins in the previous three seasons combined, and it keeps them in a tie for fifth place in the league.

But just as importantly, it allowed Indiana to conclude what had been a difficult season of road games with a victory. The Hoosiers were 2-6 in Big Ten road games coming into Sunday and had posted their worst performance of the season in a 78-66 loss at Iowa last Sunday.

The Hoosiers' fifth overall road win of the season makes for a major confidence booster heading into the regular season's final week.

"It's big for us," junior forward Christian Watford said. "It solidifies that we can get a road win. That's something that people have been talking about that we really needed. We came out here and got that tonight."

They got it in large part because they adjusted to those two opening 3-pointers. Both of those 3s — the first by sophomore Austin Hollins and the second by freshman Andre Hollins — came because the Hoosiers double-teamed senior center Ralph Sampson III, who found a shooter open.

"We just left them two wide open shots doubling down on Sampson," junior guard Jordan Hulls said. "He's a good player. He's gonna kick it

out to the open man. We had to wait for him to put it on the ground and do different things that way and be able to match up with our man."

The rest of the way, the Hoosiers did that brilliantly. The Golden Gophers were mostly without junior point guard Julian Welch, their second leading scorer, who played just 11 minutes and was limited because of a hip pointer. Watford showed his versatility by defending everyone from point guard Andre Hollins to the 6-11 Sampson. Watford and freshman forward Cody Zeller combined to hold Sampson to a maddening 1-for-11 outing and just four points.

Using Watford at the point allowed the Hoosiers to use top defenders Victor Oladipo and Will Sheehey on Minnesota's leading scorer, Rodney Williams. The 6-foot-7, 205-pounder came into the game averaging 11.0 points per contest but took just two shots and finished with three points.

Austin Hollins scored 14 points and was the only Gopher in double figures, as Minnesota (17-12, 5-11) shot just 31 percent (18-for-58) from the field. That's the second-worst performance by an Indiana opponent in Big Ten play with only Purdue (29.6 percent) experiencing more offensive futility.

"They were up in us," Austin Hollins said. "They were just fighting. Fighting hard to keep us from getting the ball. Getting over screens and switching. Just making basketball plays."

Said Crean: "We game-planned really hard for their team. When you can do that and put some different matchups that they have to adjust to, that only makes us better."

With the defense working at a high level, the Hoosiers were able to win comfortably despite getting just seven points from Zeller, who was held to single digits for just the fourth time in his freshman season. Four other players reached double figures, however, as Hulls and Watford broke out of their recent slumps with 12 points each, and Oladipo also had 12 to go with eight rebounds. Senior guard Verdell Jones III had 11 points and three assists, as the Hoosiers shot 21-for-48 from the field, 6-for-12 from 3 and 21-for-25 from the free throw line.

"We have to get to the foul line," Crean said. "There's no way around that. We have to get to the foul line. That's where we're successful. When we win, we shoot 27 free throws. When we lose, we shoot 13. And we almost got there. That's a tried and true number for us."

Shortly after the 9-0 run that gave Indiana the lead, they went on a 9-2 spurt to make it 28-18 and led 37-26 going into halftime. They posted another 9-2 run out of the break to make it 46-28. Minnesota was never closer than 16 after that, and the Hoosiers left The Barn with a road win and revenge.

(Above) The Hoosier bench watches Indiana on defense during the Indiana Minnesota basketball game.

(Right) Indiana Hoosiers guard Verdell Jones III (12) gets pumped after being fouled and Indiana Hoosiers forward Will Sheehey (10) pats him on the back.

(Below) Indiana Hoosiers guard Verdell Jones III (12) drives the ball around Minnesota Golden Gophers forward/center Ralph Sampson III (50).

INDIANA 69

	Min	3PFG	AFG	FT	O-R	A	PF	Pts
Watford, f	28	1- 1	2- 4	7- 7	2- 6	1	3	12
Sheehey, g	20	0- 1	2- 4	3- 4	2- 3	0	4	7
Zeller, f	18	0- 0	3- 8	1- 3	1- 2	1	4	7
Hulls, g	28	2- 4	4- 8	2- 2	0- 2	3	1	12
Oladipo, g	28	0- 0	4- 7	4- 4	1- 8	1	1	12
Barnett	1	0- 0	0- 0	0- 0	0- 0	0	0	0
Moore	1	0- 0	0- 0	0- 0	0- 0	0	0	0
Jones	24	1- 1	4- 7	2- 3	0- 7	3	0	11
Etherington	3	0- 0	0- 1	0- 0	0- 1	0	0	0
Abell	5	0- 0	0- 0	2- 2	0- 0	0	1	2
Howard	1	0- 0	0- 0	0- 0	0- 0	0	1	0
Pritchard	13	0- 0	0- 1	0- 0	1- 3	1	2	0
Roth	16	1- 4	1- 4	0- 0	0- 0	0	0	3
Elston	14	1- 1	1- 4	0- 0	1- 5	1	1	3
team					3- 4			
Totals		6-12	21-48	21-25	11-41	11	18	69
Shooting		.500	.438	.840				

MINNESOTA 50

	Min	3PFG	AFG	FT	O-R	A	PF	Pts
Williams, f	24	0- 1	1- 2	1- 2	0- 4	0	3	3
Sampson, f	23	0- 0	1-11	2- 3	1- 3	2	2	4
An.Hollins, g	16	2- 4	2- 6	0- 0	1- 3	0	5	6
Coleman, g	28	0- 0	2- 8	0- 0	0- 1	2	3	4
Au.Hollins, g	34	3- 5	4- 8	3- 4	2- 2	1	1	14
Welch	11	1- 3	1- 4	0- 0	0- 0	0	0	3
Osenieks	18	0- 2	1- 8	1- 3	1- 2	1	0	3
Ahanmisi	10	0- 0	0- 0	0- 0	0- 1	4	0	0
Armelin	18	1- 2	2- 6	0- 0	3- 7	0	0	5
Ingram	10	0- 0	1- 2	0- 2	3- 5	1	2	2
Eliason	8	0- 0	3- 3	0- 0	0- 2	0	4	6
team					5- 6			
Totals		7-17	18-58	7-14	16-36	11	20	50
Shooting		.412	.310	.500				

Indiana (22-7)	28	38—66
Minnesota (17-12)	26	24—50

Blocks: Indiana 5 (Watford, Zeller, Hulls, Oladipo, Jones), Minnesota 2 (Sampson, Coleman). **Turnovers:** Indiana 14 (Oladipo 5, Jones 4, Zeller 3, Watford, team), Minnesota 16 (Williams 3, Au.Hollins 3, Armelin 3, Eliason 2, Sampson, An.Hollins, Coleman, Welch, Ahanmisi). **Steals:** Indiana 5 (Oladipo 2, Watford, Zeller, Hulls), Minnesota 8 (Au.Hollins 2, Welch 2, Williams, An.Hollins, Coleman, Ingram). **Officials:** Mike Sanzere, Tom Eads, Mark Whitehead. **A:** 11,421.

Indiana Hoosiers forward Will Sheehey (10) and Indiana Hoosiers guard Remy Abell (23) celebrate the Hoosier win.

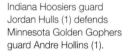

Indiana Hoosiers guard Jordan Hulls (1) defends Minnesota Golden Gophers guard Andre Hollins (1).

Indiana Hoosiers forward Christian Watford (2) grabs the rebound during the Indiana Michigan State men's basketball game at Assembly Hall in Bloomington, Ind., Tuesday, Feb. 28, 2012. Indiana won 70-55.

IU Rocks the Hall Again

Hoosiers' 70-55 win over Spartans third vs. top 5 team at home this season

By Dustin Dopirak

Apparently, the power of Assembly Hall hasn't dissipated at all since the magical days of December for Indiana. When it's packed and deafening, the old arena on 17th Street still has an ability to lift this resurgent Hoosier squad to otherworldly levels when there's a top-ranked opponent in the building. It's held true even after the Hoosiers slugged their way through the highs and lows of a rigorous Big Ten schedule.

Because three top 5 teams have now come into Assembly Hall this season, and all three have suffered defeats.

Tuesday's was the most resounding.

The No. 18 Hoosiers attacked from the opening moments and drilled a No. 5 Michigan State team that had won seven straight to clinch at least a share of the Big Ten regular season title. The 70-55 victory came in front of a packed house of 17,280 at striped-out Assembly Hall, and when it was over, IU coach Tom Crean took to the microphone to tell those fans that they'd just witnessed history.

Only one other Indiana squad in history had beaten three top 5 teams in the Associated Press poll, he told a crowd that became too loud to discern what he was saying. That was the 1975-76 team that didn't lose to anyone. Even that national championship team needed the NCAA Tournament to do it, as no other IU squad had ever pulled it off in the regular season.

It gave Crean yet another opportunity to invite the fans to bask in the joy of a season in which Indiana returned to at least relevance if not yet glory following the blue-blood program's descent to rock bottom following the Kelvin Sampson recruiting scandal. After finishing 28-66 in Crean's first three years, the Hoosiers are 23-7 overall, 10-7 in the Big Ten with wins over teams that were ranked No. 1 (Kentucky), No. 2 (Ohio State) and No. 5 (Michigan State).

"This program's been through a lot," sophomore guard Victor Oladipo said. "My first year here was real tough. I just feel as though this program deserves a lot more than we've been getting the last few years. For us to get these three big wins is one season is huge for the program, and it's huge for us, and it's huge for our confidence and things of that nature. I feel as though we deserved it."

They did, and it was in large part because they picked up on what was wrong with them nine days prior when they played a clunker of a game in a lost at Iowa and also when they lost at Michigan State. They were too passive during some of those stretches. They needed to attack and never let up.

"We can't come out lackadaisical and come out with that almost softness," senior guard Verdell Jones III said. "When we beat top teams like that, we're nasty, we're scrappy, we're fighting. I just don't think we can come out like we did against Iowa and expect that we can win. We have to have that nasty attitude every time we play."

They came out with and they sustained it in every facet. Indiana's defensive effort was perhaps the best it has been all season. Michigan State senior forward Draymond Green, who gave voters even more reason to name him Big Ten Player of the Year, had 29 points on 10-for-17 shooting and eight rebounds, but he accounted for more than half of the Spartans' points and exactly half of their field goals.

No one else on the Michigan State squad had more than eight points. The team shot 39.2 percent (20-for-51) as a team, and the Spartans outside of Green were 10-for-34.

The Hoosiers won the battle on the glass 31-30 and kept the Spartans from scoring a single second-chance point. That's no small feat considering that Michigan State has a reputation as one of the toughest teams in college basketball and came into the game ranked third in Division I in rebounding margin. Junior forward Christian Watford had a career-high 14 of those, and had a brilliant defensive effort on both Green and point guard Keith Appling.

"Possession by possession, we battled them," Crean said. "That's what you have to do to beat them. Because I think he thrives on it, meaning (coach Tom Izzo) when the other team doesn't. They thrive on it. And they're not used to 40 minutes of people being willing to battle them, because it's hard to do. Tonight was a night that we did that."

They also got the sort of across-the-board offensive contributions and harmony that they were getting early in the season when the started 15-1. Freshman forward Cody Zeller scored 18 points, showing that he had learned a lot about the physicality of the Big Ten from his first meeting with the Spartans. He scored in the post and also got out in transition with an emphatic steal and fast-break dunk that stemmed a Michigan State rally.

Oladipo attacked off the dribble with abandon scored 13 points and Jones did the same to score 12. Watford had 10 scoring inside and outside, and junior guard Jordan Hulls knocked down a pair of cold-blooded 3-pointers to finish with 10 points.

There were brief moments of stagnation, but for the most part, the Hoosiers' collective foot never came off the gas.

"We've been aggressive all year," Hulls said. "But tonight we played it for 40 minutes straight. That was a big thing for us to be able to do that." After Michigan State took a 4-1 lead to start the game, IU followed with a 17-4 run and led the rest of the way. The Spartans cut it to four in the first half and were as close as six in the second half, but the Hoosiers outscored Michigan State 11-4 in the final 5:36 to make history.

But Crean made a point to say this milestone isn't the last one. "This team still has a lot of basketball left to play," he said. "And I really believe that."

The Indiana bench reacts to a Indiana Hoosiers guard Jordan Hulls (1) 3-pointer.

MICHIGAN STATE 55

	Min	3PFG	AFG	FT	O-R	A	PF	Pts
Green, f	36	3-6	10-17	6-7	4-8	2	3	29
Payne, c	10	0-0	1-2	0-0	1-2	0	2	2
Appling, g	32	0-1	2-6	2-2	0-1	5	1	6
Thornton, g	28	2-2	3-4	0-0	0-1	1	1	8
Sawson, g	20	0-0	1-3	1-4	0-2	1	1	3
Byrd	1	0-0	0-0	0-0	0-0	0	0	0
Gauna	4	0-0	0-2	0-0	0-1	0	2	0
Kearney	10	0-1	0-1	0-0	0-1	1	0	2
Trice	8	0-2	1-4	0-0	0-1	1	0	2
Nix	26	0-0	2-7	1-2	1-4	0	1	5
Wood	25	0-1	0-5	0-2	4-7	0	2	0
team					1-2			
Totals		5-13	20-51	10-17	13-30	9	16	55
Shooting		.385	.392	.588				

INDIANA 70

	Min	3PFG	AFG	FT	O-R	A	PF	Pts
Watford, f	33	2-4	4-11	0-0	3-14	1	2	10
Sheehey, f	24	0-0	2-4	0-0	1-2	2	4	4
Zeller, c	32	0-0	7-12	4-5	2-4	1	1	18
Hulls, g	30	2-5	3-7	2-2	1-2	2	1	10
Oladipo, g	29	0-0	3-6	7-8	1-3	0	4	13
Jones	24	0-0	3-5	6-7	1-4	2	1	12
Abell	3	0-0	0-0	0-0	0-0	0	0	0
Pritchard	8	0-0	0-0	0-0	0-1	0	3	0
Roth	10	1-2	1-2	0-0	0-0	0	1	3
Elston	7	0-0	0-1	0-0	0-0	0	0	0
team					0-1			
Totals		5-11	23-48	19-22	9-31	8	16	70
Shooting		.455	.479	.864				

Indiana Hoosiers forward Christian Watford (2) is introduced.

Michigan State (24-6)	28	28—55
Indiana (23-7)	41	29—70

Blocks: Michigan State 1 (Payne), Indiana 2 (Watford, Zeller). **Turnovers:** Michigan State 13 (Green 6, Appling 3, Nix 2, Payne, Dawson), Indiana 9 (Oladipo 3, Elston 2, Sheehey, Zeller, Hulls, Jones). **Steals:** Michigan State 5 (Green 2, Payne, Appling, Nix), Indiana 10 (Hulls 3, Watford 2, Zeller 2, Oladipo 2, Jones). **Officials:** Mike Kitts, Gene Steratore, Tom O'Neill. **A:** 17, 280.

54

Indiana Hoosiers forward Christian Watford (2) blocks the shot of Michigan State Spartans forward Draymond Green (23).

Indiana Hoosiers forward Tom Pritchard (25) pulls down the rebound.

Head coach Tom Crean addresses the fans after the game.

Indiana Hoosiers forward Cody Zeller (40) goes up for the tip off.

Indiana Hoosiers guard Verdell Jones III (12) drives the baseline against Purdue Boilermakers guard Ryne Smith (24) during the Indiana Purdue men's basketball game at Assembly Hall in Bloomington, Ind., Sunday, March 4, 2012.

Fitting Finale for Hoosiers, Seniors

IU heads into postseason off win over rival Boilers

INDIANA 85
PURDUE 74

ASSEMBLY HALL
BLOOMINGTON, INDIANA

By Dustin Dopirak

The last game in Assembly Hall in Indiana's enchanted season of renewal couldn't have ended any other way, could it? It certainly would've spoiled the narrative some if the Hoosiers would've suffered their second loss in Bloomington this year and for it to happen against their in-state rival. And it certainly wouldn't have been quite as sweet for Indiana if the Hoosiers weren't able to send in together in the game's final minute their five seniors, the ones who willingly signed up to rebuild a kingdom in ruin and finally got to see it rise again in their final season.

But the Hoosiers' 85-74 win over Purdue in front of 17,472 at Assembly Hall made sure this chapter of the story book ended the way the fairy tale writers would have it. Despite a second-half charge from the Boilermakers that was just enough to make the Hoosiers nervous, the double-digit lead in the final minute allowed Indiana to check in seniors Kory Barnett, Verdell Jones III, Daniel Moore, Tom Pritchard and Matt Roth with 22 seconds to go, as they exchanged hugs with each other and all five players who were coming off the floor to allow them their Assembly Hall swan song.

"It's a special feeling," Jones said. "It's something I'm going to definitely remember. Just walking off together. Beating our rival and a sold-out crowd. That's a great feeling."

Said Indiana coach Tom Crean: "It's a fitting day. It's a fitting day for these guys to have a win like this. To beat a rival like this, to beat a team that was arguably playing as well as anyone in the last couple of weeks. And not just in the Big Ten, but around the country."

The win over the Boilermakers is important for the Hoosiers' standing in a number of ways heading into Thursday's Big Ten Tournament. The win clinches Indiana (24-7 overall, 11-7 in the Big Ten) the No. 5 seed and a date against No. 12 Penn State at approximately 2 p.m. on Thursday at Bankers Life Fieldhouse in Indianapolis. It also gave the Hoosiers their eighth win over an opponent currently in the top 50 of the Ratings Percentage Index, which bolsters their resume for NCAA Tournament seeding even further. It allows them to close out the season at Assembly Hall with an 18-1 record.

But it also makes for another feat that this Hoosier team will get to keep with it for eternity, and one that that will mean more to it than many others because of the depths Indiana has seen since 2008 and the way their rivals have taken advantage of them. It means the Hoosiers swept the state, beating Purdue twice in the same season for the first time since 2006 while claiming wins against Evansville, Butler and Notre Dame.

"This rivalry is often overlooked because of the North Carolina-Duke rivalry, but I think this is the best rivalry in college basketball," Jones said. "Just to be able to beat them and come in and sweep the state of Indiana, it's a great feeling."

The Hoosiers were able to do it without much drama on Sunday because they had scoring coming from everywhere in the first half like they did back in November and December. They got at least three field goals from six players in the first half, as well as a 3-pointer and three assists from junior point guard Jordan Hulls. They shot a scalding 20-for-30 (67 percent) in the first half, including 8-for-14 from beyond the arc. Roth hit all three of his 3-pointers in the half, and sophomore swingman Will Sheehey, who hadn't hit a 3-pointer since Feb. 9, knocked down two and scored 11 points. The Hoosiers had 12 assists on their 20 field goals, committing just five turnovers.

Their 49 first-half points were second only to the 54 they had against Iowa for the most the Hoosiers had in the first half against a Big Ten opponent this season. They went on a 15-6 run to start the game, then a 13-4 spurt to take a 15-point lead and were up 49-31 at halftime.

"We just wanted to come out being aggressive and that's what we did," Hulls said. "We were able to knock a lot of shots in. That's just moving the ball around and playing good defense and creating turnovers and getting fast break points."

The Hoosiers weren't nearly as hot from the field in the second half — shooting 8-for-23 (34.8 percent) — and they also got sloppy on defense, allowing Purdue to shoot 52 percent (16-for-31) while also knocking down four 3-pointers. However they continued to keep the Purdue at an arm's length, hitting 18 of 23 free throws in the second half.

The Hoosiers finished with four scorers in double figures. Junior forward Christian Watford led the group with 19 points as well as six rebounds and two assists. Sheehey scored 16 points, breaking double figures in a conference game for the first time since the Iowa game on Jan. 29. Freshman forward Cody Zeller had 13 points and seven rebounds, and Hulls finished with 10 points and five assists against just one turnover.

Purdue actually put five in double figures. Senior point guard Lewis Jackson scored 17, senior forward Robbie Hummel had 16. Sophomore guard Terone Johnson had 13 points and sharpshooters Ryne Smith and D.J. Byrd had 12 each.

All of that allowed the Boilermakers to cut the deficit to as few as six points with 1:20 to, but the Hoosiers knocked down enough free throws from that point on to keep it from getting any closer.

And that assured that the Hoosiers head into the Big Ten Tournament with a four-game winning streak and seven wins in their last eight games, which should presumably mean momentum.

"It's good as long as they keep understanding why they have it," Crean said. "Our guys need to keep understanding why they're being successful."

And why there was so much magic at Assembly Hall in 2011-12.

Seniors Indiana Hoosiers forward Kory Barnett (0) and Indiana Hoosiers guard Daniel Moore (11) enter the game.

Indiana Hoosiers forward Cody Zeller (40) swats at the rebound as Purdue Boilermakers guard Terone Johnson (0) pulls it down.

PURDUE 74

	Min	3PFG	AFG	FT	O-	R	A	PF	Pts
Hummel, f	35	2- 2	7-12	0- 0	0- 8		1	5	16
Carroll, f	24	0- 0	1- 3	0- 1	1- 1		0	3	2
TJohnson, g	27	0- 1	5-10	3- 4	1- 4		1	2	13
Jackson, g	34	0- 0	6-12	5- 6	22- 5		3	2	17
Smith, g	31	4- 7	4- 9	0- 0	0- 2		1	1	12
AJohnson	13	0- 0	1- 3	0- 0	0- 2		0	3	2
Byrd	30	2-10	4-14	2- 2	3- 5		3	4	12
Hart	6	0- 1	0- 1	0- 0	0- 0		2	2	0
team					2- 4				
Totals		8-21	28-64	10-13	9-31		11	22	74
Shooting		.381	.438	.769					

INDIANA 85

	Min	3PFG	AFG	FT	O-	R	A	PF	Pts
Watford, f	29	1- 2	6- 9	6- 6	0- 6		2	3	19
Sheehey, f	29	3- 4	5- 7	3- 4	3- 5		0	3	16
Zeller, c	29	0- 0	4- 6	5- 8	2- 7		1	3	13
Hulls, g	32	2- 4	3- 7	2- 2	0- 2		5	1	10
Oladipo, g	25	0- 1	3- 6	3- 4	0- 8		3	1	9
Barnett	1	0- 0	0- 0	0- 0	0- 0		0	0	0
Moore	1	0- 0	0- 0	0- 0	0- 0		0	0	0
Jones	21	1- 1	3- 5	0- 0	0- 2		2	1	7
Abell	1	0- 0	0- 0	0- 0	0- 0		0	0	0
Pritchard	9	0- 1	1- 4	0- 1	0- 0		1	0	2
Roth	15	3- 3	3- 3	0- 0	0- 1		0	1	9
Elston	8	0- 2	0- 6	0- 0	1- 3		2	1	0
team					1- 3				
Totals		10-18	28-53	19-25	7-37		16	14	85
Shooting		.556	.528	.760					

Purdue (20-11, 10-8 Big Ten)	34	40—74	
Indiana (24-7, 11-7)	49	36—85	

Blocks: Purdue 1 (Hart), Indiana 5 (Zeller 2, Jones 2, Oladipo). **Turnovers:** Purdue 10 (TJohnson 3, Jackson 2, Hummel, Carroll, Smith, AJohnson, Byrd), Indiana 12 (Watford 3, Zeller 2, Oladipo 2, Hulls, Moore, Jones, Roth, team). **Steals:** Purdue 8 (Carroll 2, Jackson 2, Hummel, TJohnson, Smith, Byrd), Indiana 6 (Hulls 2, Jones 2, Zeller, Pritchard). **Officials:** Ed Hightower, Jim Burr, Mike Whitehead. **A:** 17,472.

Indiana Hoosiers forward Will Sheehey (10) celebrates a 3-pointer just before they head to timeout.

Indiana Hoosiers forward Will Sheehey (10) lays the ball in over Purdue Boilermakers forward Robbie Hummel (4).

Seniors Indiana Hoosiers forward Kory Barnett (0), Indiana Hoosiers guard Daniel Moore (11) and Indiana Hoosiers forward Tom Pritchard (25) check into the game.

Indiana Hoosiers guard Jordan Hulls (1) lays the ball in during the Indiana Penn State men's basketball game at the Big Ten Tournament at Banker's Life Fieldhouse in Indianapolis, Ind., Thursday, March 8, 2012. Indiana won 75-58.

Hoosier Victory Rings Hollow

INDIANA 75
PENN STATE 58

BANKERS LIFE FIELDHOUSE
INDIANAPOLIS, INDIANA

Jones' injury spoils IU's first Big Ten tournament win since 2006

By Dustin Dopirak

Even though it was expected, this was a win Indiana should've been able to bask in. The fifth-seeded Hoosiers' 75-58 victory over No. 12 seed Penn State in front of 17,936 at Bankers Life Fieldhouse in the first round of the Big Ten Tournament represented yet another milestone for this resurgent squad.

It was Indiana's first Big Ten Tournament victory since 2006, a slump that not only included the first three seasons of the Tom Crean era but also both of Kelvin Sampson's years at the helm. But the tears Crean was fighting back in postgame interviews were not tears of joy. Indiana couldn't enjoy the victory quite as much, because someone who had seen all the tough times was missing from the bench at game's end.

Senior guard Verdell Jones III, the 23rd leading scorer in program history, injured his knee with 5:45 to go in the first half, had to be carried off the floor and never returned. "Without a doubt, it's a tough afternoon," Crean said. "You want to win, which we did. You want to play well. But you want to do it with your whole team, but we didn't get to do that today."

Jones drove to the free throw line and came to a jump stop with the intent to either take a jumper or at least make a shot fake. His right knee buckled underneath him, however, and he went to the floor immediately. The official word from Indiana was that he had suffered a knee sprain and would continue to be evaluated.

However, Crean did not sound optimistic about a swift return.

"He's being evaluated now," Crean said in his post-game press conference. "... I was hopeful when he went down that it wasn't as significant. I'm going to keep holding out that hope, but I don't obviously feel good about that. We've prayed numerous times. It's in the doctors' hands. It's in God's hands. We're just going to absolutely hope for the best for him."

A sprained ligament is the same as a torn ligament, it's just a question of severity.

Jones won't have much time to recover, even if he can return. Crean said freshman guard Remy Abell will be used to fill his minutes, but the void Jones leaves is much greater than that. Jones averages 7.8 points per game and is second on the team with 94 assists. He's effectively co-captained the Hoosiers with junior point guard Jordan Hulls. He's the most visible member of a senior class that joined the program after the Kelvin Sampson recruiting sanctions and subsequent roster purge and played through three of the most trying seasons in program history.

It was devastating for Crean to see Jones go down so close to the program's first NCAA Tournament appearance since 2008. At 25-7, the Hoosiers are beyond a lock to get in, and at this point are just playing for seeding.

"We go through a lot together," Crean said. "With these guys, we go through a lot together. Verdell Jones III stands a lot for what's right here. When you start to think about all of the things that these seniors have had to endure and go through, and now to be at this point, that's tough. That's a tough blow. ... just watching him in pain. That's hard. There's no worse feeling than when your children are sick or hurt. It's really a lot like that when you coach."

Instead of letting the emotion of the moment get to them, though, Indiana responded quickly after Jones went down and took control of the game. Senior guard Matt Roth knocked down a 3-pointer eight seconds after play resumed, starting a 7-0 run that gave the Hoosiers a 31-21 lead with 4:05 left in the half. Penn State cut it to 38-32 at half, but Indiana went on a 14-0 run early in the second half to go up 54-34 with 12:27 to go and cruise the rest of the way. Both teams had rough shooting nights with the Hoosiers finishing 19-for-52 (36.5 percent), and Penn State shooting slightly worse at 19-for-55 (34.5 percent). However, the Hoosiers got a sublime performance from Hulls, who had experience at Bankers Life Fieldhouse (back when it was still Conseco) during Bloomington South's state championship run in 2009 as well as Indiana's game against Notre Dame earlier this year. He seemed to have mastered the deceptive shooting backdrop right out of the gate, finishing 7-for-10 from the field and 4-for-6 from beyond the 3-point arc for a team-high 20 points.

"Shots were falling down for me," Hulls said. "Teammates were finding me when I was open, and I was able to create a little bit on my own."

The rest of the squad was a combined 12-for-42, but the guys who weren't shooting well were at least making their free throws. Junior forward Christian Watford was 2-for-11 from the field but a perfect 10-for-10 from the foul line for 14 points to go with 10 rebounds. Freshman forward Cody Zeller was 4-for-9, but he made 11 of his 15 foul shots and also posted a double-double with 19 points and 10 rebounds.

Sophomore guard Victor Oladipo was just 1-for-8 from the field, but he also grabbed 10 rebounds, and the Hoosiers won the rebounding battle 45-29.

Defensively, they simply wore out Penn State junior point guard Tim Frazier. The All-Big Ten first-teamer finished with 26 points and four assists, but he was 9-for-24 from the field and scored just seven of those points in the second half on 2-for-10 shooting. The Hoosiers used just about every defensive look they could think of, marking him with at least five different man-to-man defenders, but also using a lot of 2-3 zone to clog the lane and bottle him up. "Different players went on him, I went on him, Will (Sheehey) went on him, and we went zone," Oladipo said. "Just showing him different looks and I think that slowed him down a little in the second half."

Said Hulls: "We just had to keep him in front. I think the 2-3 zone really helped us out. Just a different show of defense for him. He was able to find some guys sometimes, but overall I think we did a lot better job in the second half."

Guard Trey Lewis was the only other Penn State player in double figures with 11 points, so with Frazier slumping there was little else the Nittany Lions (12-20) could do offensively. After the Hoosiers went up by 20, Penn State was never within 13 and the Hoosiers advanced without much more drama.

"It's been a long time coming," junior forward Christian Watford said. "And we're going to enjoy it."

Just not as much as they would have with Jones.

(Right and Below) Indiana Hoosiers guard Verdell Jones III (12) plants to take a shot and his knee gives out.

PENN STATE 58

	Min	3PFG	AFG	FT	O- R	A	PF	Pts
Graham, f	23	0- 0	1- 5	0- 1	3- 7	1	3	2
Travis, f	21	0- 0	2- 5	2- 4	3- 7	0	4	6
Lewis, g	26	3- 7	4- 9	0- 0	0- 1	2	5	11
Marshall, g	38	1- 3	1- 6	6- 7	0- 4	0	4	9
Frazier, g	39	4- 6	9-24	4- 4	0- 2	4	4	26
Glover	30	0- 0	0- 2	0- 0	1- 3	1	5	0
Montminy	1	0- 0	0- 0	0- 0	0- 0	0	0	0
Colella	6	0- 1	0- 1	0- 0	0- 0	0	0	0
Borovnjnak	14	0- 0	2- 3	0- 0	2- 3	0	3	4
Ackerman	1	0- 0	0- 0	0- 0	0- 0	0	0	0
Wisniewski	1	0- 0	0- 0	0- 0	0- 0	0	0	0
team					1- 2			
Totals		8-17	19-55	12-16	10-29	8	28	58
Shooting		.471	.345	.750				

INDIANA 75

	Min	3PFG	AFG	FT	O- R	A	PF	Pts
Watford, f	33	0- 2	2-11	10-10	2-10	2	2	14
Zeller, f	31	0- 0	4- 9	11-15	7-10	2	2	19
Hulls, g	31	4- 6	7-10	2- 2	0- 0	1	2	20
Oladipo, g	32	0- 1	1- 8	3- 4	2-10	2	3	5
Sheehey, g	27	1- 3	2- 7	0- 1	0- 3	2	0	5
Barnett	1	0- 0	0- 0	0- 0	0- 0	0	0	0
Moore	1	0- 0	0- 0	0- 0	0- 0	0	0	0
Jones	6	0- 0	0- 0	0- 0	0- 1	1	0	0
Etherington	2	0- 0	0- 0	0- 0	0- 0	0	0	0
Abell	6	0- 0	1- 2	2- 2	0- 1	0	0	2
Pritchard	10	0- 0	0- 0	0- 0	2- 2	0	3	0
Roth	14	2- 5	2- 5	0- 0	0- 0	1	2	6
Elston	6	1- 1	1- 1	1- 2	0- 1	0	1	4
team					5- 7			
Totals		8-18	19-52	29-36	16-45	11	16	75
Shooting		.444	.365	.806				

Penn State (12-20)	32	26	—58
Indiana (25-7)	38	37	—75

Blocks: Penn State 8 (Ross 3, Graham 2, Marshall 2, Frazier), Indiana 2 (Oladipo, Zeller). **Turnovers:** Penn State 10 (Frazier 4, Glover 2, Marshall, Travis, Borovnjak, team), Indiana 11 (Oladipo 3, Hulls 2, Sheehey 2, Jones 2, Zeller, team). **Steals:** Penn State 8 (Frazier 5, Lewis, Marshall, Glover), Indiana 4 (Hulls, Oladipo, Sheehey, Zeller). **Officials:** Ed Hightower, Ray Perone, D.J. Carstensen. **A:** 17,936.

(Right) Indiana Hoosiers forward Cody Zeller (40) grabs the pass.

(Below) Indiana Hoosiers forward Kory Barnett (0) celebrates with the Hoosier bench as they started strong in the second period.

Indiana Hoosiers forward Cody Zeller (40) manages to keep control of the ball and hit the bucket as Wisconsin Badgers forward Mike Bruesewitz (31) defends during the Indiana Wisconsin men's basketball game at the Big Ten Tournament at Banker's Life Fieldhouse in Indianapolis, Ind., Friday, March 9, 2012.

Badgers Shoot Down IU

Unheralded Wilson pours in 30 points as Wisconsin KOs Hoosiers

By Dustin Dopirak

Of course the dagger came from Rob Wilson. How else could this one have possibly ended? On just about every previous occasion in the second half when Indiana threatened to finally erase Wisconsin's lead, the previously anonymous Wisconsin senior guard stepped up with a huge shot to knock the Hoosiers' back. It was only fitting that he would hit the shot to bury them.

And that was exactly what happened with 35 seconds to go when Wilson swished a rainbow 3-pointer to give the Badgers a 72-65 lead, effectively crushing the Hoosiers' hopes in the quarterfinals of the Big Ten Tournament. That shot gave Wilson, who came into the game averaging 3.1 points per game, a career high 30 points, and the Badgers hit enough free throws to take a 79-71 victory in front of 18,484 at Bankers Life Fieldhouse and advance to today's 1:40 p.m. semifinal against Michigan State.

The Hoosiers (25-8) now await Selection Sunday for their NCAA Tournament fate. They will almost certainly be a top-5 seed and are currently slotted as a No. 4 seed by most bracket experts, but winning this one might have put them in line for a No. 3 seed.

"We had some guys play very well," Indiana coach Tom Crean said. "They had some guys play very well. The difference was Rob Wilson played tremendous."

Crean said the Hoosiers saw reason to be concerned about Wilson in his previous four games, which included his lone double-digit scoring effort of the season when he scored 11 points, and the Badgers' win over Ohio State when he hit three 3-pointers for nine points. However, there was very little in Wilson's past at Wisconsin that suggested he was capable of this.

The 6-foot-4, 200-pound Cleveland native has never averaged more than 12.2 minutes or 3.1 points per game in a season. His previous career scoring high was 13 points against Michigan in 2010, and last season with his minutes limited with a hamstring injury he scored a total of 36 points in the season.

But Wilson hit two 3-pointers in the first seven minutes Friday, and he knew he was on. He finished 11-for-16 from the field, more than doubling his previous career high of five field goals in a game. He was 7-for-10 from beyond the 3-point arc, more than doubling his previous career high of three made 3s.

"The weight of the ball felt like it was going in today," Wilson said. "I don't remember that feeling in a long time."

Said Wisconsin coach Bo Ryan: "Needless to say, we had a player who was in the zone."

And in the second half especially, every shot took some of the air out of Indiana's comeback.

The Hoosiers fell behind 28-17 in the first half but had cut the deficit to 42-41 with 15:40 to go in the second half after sophomore guard Victor Oladipo made one of two free throws off an intentional foul by Wisconsin's Jordan Taylor.

However, Oladipo turned the ball over, and Wilson hit back-to-back 3-pointers to make it 48-41. Indiana followed with a 6-0 run to make it a one-point game again, but then Wilson hit a 3 with 12:44 to go to make it a two-possession game again. IU junior guard Jordan Hulls hit two free throws to make it 51-49, but Taylor hit a 3-pointer, then Wilson made another 3 to make it 57-50.

And of course, when the Hoosiers were within four with a minute to go and clinging to life, Wilson hit that final 3-pointer to put the game away.

"Every time we were close to getting momentum going back our way, they made a big play," Crean said. "And it was usually Rob Wilson making that play."

Crean and the Hoosiers gave Wilson credit for making the shots, but they admitted they were certainly culpable in springing him for a scoring night beyond at least any of his realistic dreams. There were too many occasions when they left him open by helping on drives or in the post. There were too many times when they went under screens or had other miscommunications that kept them from properly contesting his shots.

"Rob Wilson was fully accounted for in the way that we prepared," Crean said. "It just didn't look that way today, and he got really, really hot, and we didn't do a great job of taking him away. Some of the 3s, he earned them, and others he made because he was open because we over-helped on the ball."

Said freshman forward Cody Zeller: "We knew that he could shoot the ball, but we gave him too many openings. Especially once he got hot. We didn't change anything in our defensive strategy to get out on him more."

Wilson wasn't the only Wisconsin player to take advantage of those openings. The Badgers (24-8) hit 13 3-pointers, a season-high by an Indiana opponent. Junior forward Jared Berggren had 16 points and nine rebounds, junior forward Ryan Evans had 12 points, and senior guard Jordan Taylor had 12 despite shooting just 3-for-12 from the field. Sophomore guard Josh Gasser hit three 3-pointers for nine points and four assists.

The Hoosiers got 17 points each from Hulls, Zeller and junior forward Christian Watford, who also grabbed 10 rebounds to post his third double-double in four games.

However, the Hoosiers went long stretches without getting the ball to Zeller and Oladipo was just 2-for-12 from the field. For the first time in the Crean era, the end of the Big Ten Tournament does not mean the end of the Hoosiers season. Though the mood in the locker room after the game was downcast, they know Sunday means the start of a new season.

"We'll go back, and we'll get together I'm sure, and we'll be ready to figure out where we're going and who we're playing," Watford said. "And we'll continue to move forward."

But an unknown Wisconsin senior stopped their forward progress for a day.

Head coach Tom Crean reacts to the charge foul called on Indiana Hoosiers forward Derek Elston (32).

(Right) Indiana Hoosiers guard Jordan Hulls (1) pulls his teammates together after Indiana Hoosiers guard Victor Oladipo (4) committed a foul.

(Below, left) Indiana Hoosiers forward Cody Zeller (40) defends Wisconsin Badgers forward/center Jared Berggren (40).

(Below, center) Indiana Hoosiers forward Christian Watford (2) goes up for the shot as Wisconsin Badgers guard/forward Ryan Evans (5) defends.

(Below, right) Indiana Hoosiers guard Verdell Jones III (12) watches his teammates warm up.

INDIANA 71

	Min	3PFG	AFG	FT	O-R	A	PF	Pts
Watford, f	29	2-3	5-10	5-5	1-10	1	2	17
Sheehey, f	31	0-1	3-4	0-0	0-2	0	2	6
Zeller, c	31	0-0	5-9	7-8	1-1	0	4	17
Hulls, g	29	1-1	7-10	2-2	1-2	2	1	17
Oladipo, g	29	0-0	2-12	3-5	3-5	4	1	7
Etherington	3	0-0	0-0	0-0	0-0	0	0	0
Abell	15	0-0	2-3	1-2	0-2	2	1	5
Pritchard	7	0-0	0-0	0-0	0-0	0	0	0
Roth	12	0-1	0-1	0-0	0-1	1	3	0
Elston	14	0-0	1-2	0-0	1-3	0	2	2
team					3-4			
Totals		3-6	25-51	18-22	10-30	8	16	71
Shooting		.500	.490	.818				

WISCONSIN 79

	Min	3PFG	AFG	FT	O-R	A	PF	Pts
Evans, f	30	0-1	5-10	2-5	1-6	1	3	12
Bruesewitz, f	22	0-1	0-1	0-0	3-4	3	2	0
Berggren, c	36	1-4	5-9	5-5	3-9	1	5	16
Taylor, g	32	2-5	3-12	4-4	2-3	4	4	12
Gaser, g	38	3-4	3-5	0-0	0-2	4	2	9
Brust	7	0-0	0-2	0-0	0-0	1	0	0
Wilson	32	7-10	11-16	1-2	1-2	1	0	30
Kaminsky	3	0-1	0-1	0-0	0-0	1	0	0
team					1-2			
Totals		13-26	27-56	12-16	11-28	16	16	79
Shooting		.500	.482	.750				

Indiana (25-8)		31	40—71
Indiana (1-0)		36	43—79

Blocks: Indiana 0, Wisconsin 2 (Evans, Berggren). **Turnovers:** Indiana 10 (Hulls 3, Watford 2, Oladipo 2, Sheehey, Zeller, Elston), Wisconsin 7 (Berggren 2, Taylor 2, team 2, Bruesewitz). **Steals:** Indiana 1 (Zeller), Wisconsin 4 (Berggren, Taylor, Gaser, Brust). **Officials:** Mike Kitts, D.J. Carstensen, Jim Schipper. A: 18,484.

(Left) Indiana Hoosiers guard/forward Will Sheehey (10) was injured while defending Wisconsin Badgers guard Jordan Taylor (11).

(Below, left) Wisconsin Badgers guard/forward Rob Wilson (33) takes the charge as Indiana Hoosiers forward Derek Elston (32) goes for the layup.

(Below) Indiana Hoosiers guard Victor Oladipo (4) attempts a layup.

IU Gets Taste of Tournament Success

Hoosiers dominate New Mexico State, 79-66, in NCAA opener

By Dustin Dopirak

Indiana got a chance to soak in the victory before it was even over. With New Mexico State having finally surrendered in the final half-minute, they dribbled out the shot clock with the sound of hundreds of Hoosiers fans chanting "I-U," celebrating the fact that Indiana would keep dancing for at least two more days.

There were moments of sloppiness for the Hoosiers in their first NCAA Tournament game since 2008, but in the end they did what they had to do to win and win comfortably. Junior point guard Jordan Hulls got hot from beyond the arc for a game-high 22 points, the No. 4 seed Hoosiers kept No. 13 New Mexico State from dominating the paint and beat the Aggies 79-66 in front of 17,519 on Thursday at The Rose Garden to advance to the third round of the NCAA Tournament. They will play No. 12 seed Virginia Commonwealth — which upset No. 5 seed Wichita State 62-59 earlier in the evening — on Saturday at 7:10 p.m.

It was their first tournament victory since March 17, 2007.

"We are extremely happy," Indiana coach Tom Crean said. "Not satisfied in the sense that we could've played better at times and there's some more basketball ahead of us, but happy to have the first game put away now. The key for us was our approach. For a team that had not been in this environment, had not been in this type of arena — and I don't just mean Rose Garden, I mean the NCAA Tournament arena, they handled it very, very well."

The Hoosiers hit on just about every goal of their game plan. They didn't want to get pounded on the glass by the Aggies, who came into the game third in Division I in rebounding margin. New Mexico State still won the rebounding battle, but not by much, 23-21. Both teams had the same amount of offensive rebounds with seven.

The Aggies also shot more free throws this season (1,048) than any other team in Division I. On Thursday, the Hoosiers sent them to the line only 10 times, where they made eight.

"That was huge for us," freshman center Cody Zeller said. "They get a lot of offensive rebounds. They get to the free throw line quite a bit. Those are two of the biggest keys. I think it prepared us playing good teams in the Big Ten like Michigan State ... I think that was a big key for us tonight and we did a fairly good job of that."

They also knew that they could push the tempo on New Mexico State, but to do that, they needed turnovers. They caused 17, which allowed them to get in transition and score 24 points off turnovers.

Zeller was responsible for many of those himself, registering six steals, an Indiana school record for an NCAA Tournament game. "I felt like I was quicker than their big guys," Zeller said. "They were probably a little bit stronger. I just tried to use my quickness when they were passing inside. I just tried to get some deflections and just tried to be active."

Beyond the obvious game plan points, the Hoosiers are always better when they're hitting from outside and getting scoring from sources outside of Zeller.

Hulls made sure that happened in a big way.

The South graduate spent most of the first half looking to facilitate, hitting one 3-pointer but also dishing out three assists.

In the second half, though, he started getting looks, and once he did, he didn't stop shooting. He finished 8-for-12 from the field, 7-for-8 in the second half, knocking down four of six 3-pointers for 22 points.

"I was just getting open looks from my teammates," Hulls said. "Whether it was off the ball screens or different things off of ball screens. I hit the first shot, then it started feeling a little bit better when it was leaving my hand and I was able to knock down some shots."

Hulls hitting opened up things for everyone else as well. Junior forward Christian Watford actually got things started with 10 points in the first half and he finished with 14. Zeller and sophomore forward Will Sheehey also scored 14 each. The Hoosiers shot 59.3 percent for the game (32-for-54) and 64.3 percent (18-for-28) in the second half.

New Mexico State was shooting at almost as good of a clip. The Aggies made 55.1 percent of their shots (27-for-49) with senior forward Wendell McKines leading the way with 15 points and seven rebounds.

However, the Hoosiers still took a double-digit lead in the first half, went into the break up 35-28, and went on a 17-5 run to take a 62-41 lead with 11:42 to go. New Mexico State got back within striking distance at 65-53, but was never closer than 12 and IU was reminded of the feel of an NCAA Tournament win.

(Opposite page) Indiana Hoosiers forward Christian Watford (2) fouls New Mexico State Aggies forward Wendell McKines (31) during the Indiana New Mexico State 2012 NCAA Men's Basketball second round game at the Rose Garden in Portland, Ore., Friday, March 15, 2012. Indiana won 79-66.

(Above) The Indiana bench celebrates a Indiana Hoosiers guard Jordan Hulls (1) 3-pointer.

(Bottom, left) Indiana Hoosiers forward Tom Pritchard (25) defends New Mexico State Aggies forward Tyrone Watson (45).

(Bottom, right) New Mexico State Aggies center Hamidu Rahman (32) and New Mexico State Aggies forward Tyrone Watson (45) manage to call a timeout before Indiana Hoosiers guard Jordan Hulls (1) could get a jump ball called on the loose ball.

NEW MEXICO STATE 66

	Min	3PFG	AFG	FT	O-R	R	A	PF	Pts
McKines, f	39	1- 3	6-10	2- 2	3- 7		1	2	15
Watson, f	31	0- 2	2- 5	2- 2	0- 1		1	1	6
Rahman, c	15	0- 0	3- 6	0- 0	1- 3		0	3	6
Laroche, g	35	1- 3	3- 9	1- 2	1- 3		2	2	8
Mullings, g	34	0- 1	5- 9	0- 0	1- 4		3	3	10
Barry	4	0- 0	0- 0	0- 0	0- 0		0	0	0
Sy	19	2- 3	5- 7	0- 0	0- 0		0	0	12
Nephawe	23	0- 0	3- 3	3- 4	0- 4		0	2	9
team					1- 1				
Totals		4-12	27-49	8-10	7-23		7	13	66
Shooting		.333	.551	.800					

INDIANA 79

	Min	3PFG	AFG	FT	O-R	R	A	PF	Pts
Watford, f	32	2- 3	6-11	0- 0	0- 4		1	2	14
Sheehey, f	32	0- 2	7-11	0- 0	2- 3		0	1	14
Zeller, c	30	0- 0	5- 9	4- 6	1- 6		4	3	14
Hulls, g	35	4- 6	8-12	2- 2	0- 2		3	2	22
Oladipo, g	31	0- 1	3- 7	0- 0	0- 1		3	0	6
Abell	17	0- 0	1- 1	2- 2	1- 1		2	0	4
Pritchard	10	0- 0	1- 1	0- 0	2- 2		1	2	2
Roth	5	0- 0	0- 0	0- 0	0- 0		0	0	0
Elston	8	1- 1	1- 2	0- 0	1- 2		1	2	3
Totals		7-13	32-54	8-10	7-21		15	12	79
Shooting		.538	.593	.800					

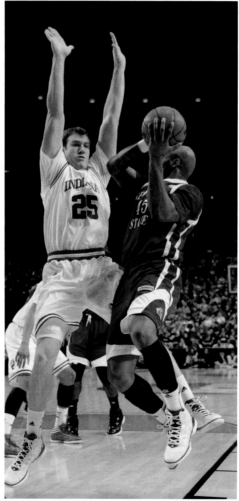

New Mexico State (26-10)	28	38—	66
Indiana (26-8)	35	44—	79

Blocks: New Mexico State 6 (Nephawe 3, Watson, McKines, Rahman), Indiana 0. **Turnovers:** New Mexico State 17 (Watson 7, Mullings 3, Rahman 3, Laroche 2, Sy, Nephawe), Indiana 12 (Pritchard 2, Watford 2, Oladipo 2, Zeller 2, Abell, Sheehey, Hulls, Elston). **Steals:** New Mexico State 5 (Laroche 2, Sy, Watson, Rahman), Indiana 12 (Zeller 6, Hulls 3, Sheehey, Pritchard, Oladipo). **Officials:** Michael Roberts, Kevin Brill, Sean Hull. **A:** 17,519.

Indiana Hoosiers guard Jordan Hulls (1) guards New Mexico State Aggies guard Hernst Laroche (13).

Indiana Hoosiers forward Christian Watford (2) celebrates the good Hoosier start on his way to a timeout after hitting a 3-pointer.

New Mexico State Aggies guard Hernst Laroche (13) pushes Indiana Hoosiers forward Cody Zeller (40) back as he defends.

Indiana fans cheer the Hoosiers on as the final seconds tick off the clock during the Indiana New Mexico State 2012 NCAA Men's Basketball second round game at the Rose Garden in Portland, Ore., Friday, March 15, 2012. Indiana won 79-66.

Indiana Hoosiers guard Victor Oladipo (4) high fives the cheerleaders and fans who were at the pep rally send off before the Indiana New Mexico State 2012 NCAA Men's Basketball second round game.

Indiana Hoosiers forward Will Sheehey (10) celebrates the Hoosier win during the Indiana Virginia Commonwealth 2012 NCAA Men's Basketball third round game at the Rose Garden in Portland, Ore., Saturday, March 17, 2012.

IU Finds a Will, and a Way

Sheehey's late bucket lift Hoosiers over VCU, 63-61

By Dustin Dopirak

Will Sheehey grabbed the ball on the left baseline after Victor Oladipo's shot was blocked and flashed an involuntary smile, because he knew.

It mattered not that the sophomore swingman was in perhaps the biggest pressure situation of his basketball career, or that the shot he was about to take could be the one that either continued Indiana's magical 2011-12 season with a dramatic late comeback or led to its eventual end. When he gets that look, that wide open, it goes in. Every time.

"Will's mid-range is almost automatic," Oladipo said. "When he shot it, I knew it was going in as soon as it left his hands."

It did, and then on the other end, Virginia Commonwealth guard Rob Brandenberg's 3-pointer for the win hit off the front of the rim — and after hanging above it for a perceived eternity — fell over the back end to give the No. 4 Hoosiers a breathtaking 63-61 NCAA Tournament victory over the No. 12 seed Rams, a berth in the Sweet 16 and a rematch with No. 1 Kentucky.

The Hoosiers had been down as many as nine points and trailed almost the entire second half. They committed 22 turnovers against VCU's vaunted full-court pressure and relentless half-court trapping. They not only needed Sheehey's jumper but a gargantuan three-point play by Oladipo in the final minute to advance.

But somehow they move on to Atlanta to play in their first Sweet 16 since 2002 and just the second for the storied program since 1995. And they're doing it all just four years after the program's implosion because of the Kelvin Sampson recruiting scandal.

"It's why we play the game," senior guard Matt Roth said. "It's why we fought through all the adversity and the ups and downs and the injuries and just kept bouncing back."

Said Oladipo: "It's great to be in here with these guys and experience it with these guys. They've been through so much. They deserve it. ... These guys are so excited, man. They deserve it, man. We didn't quit. And that's the reason why they won."

There were so many times when the Rams seemingly pushed the Hoosiers to their brink. As pesky as the full-court press was, the trapping did even more to throw Indiana's ball-handlers off their game. VCU double-teamed the ball-handler off of every ball screen, forcing Oladipo and junior guard Jordan Hulls to five turnovers each.

But the Hoosiers stayed in it because they were making just as many stops in the half-court, holding VCU to 40.4 percent shooting, and because they got several key individual performances when they absolutely needed them.

The first came just before the half. The Hoosiers were down 35-33 when Sheehey was called with a flagrant foul — after a lengthy video review — for making slight contact with the face of a VCU player with his elbow. Forward Treveon Graham hit a free throw to make it 36-33, sparking a 7-0 run that made it 42-33 with 1:47 to go.

But then Indiana junior forward Christian Watford took over, hitting back-to-back 3-pointers and then drawing a foul and hitting two free throws to make it 42-41 at halftime.

"I just knew we were at a very vulnerable point," Watford said. "I didn't want them to get up too big going into the half. I just felt like we had to do something. I got some open looks and just so happened to knock them down."

VCU went on a 9-0 run to make it 57-48 with 12:28 to go, but the Hoosiers got a tip-in from senior forward Tom Pritchard and a layup by freshman guard Remy Abell to make it a four-point game again. And in the final seven minutes, freshman forward Cody Zeller was dominant, grabbing five rebounds and scoring five points in that stretch to finish with 16 points and 13 rebounds for the game.

Zeller hit two free throws with 1:31 to go, but the Hoosiers were still behind 61-58. VCU senior guard Bradford Burgess had a chance to make it a two-possession game, but missed two critical free throws with one minute to go.

Watford grabbed a big rebound on the second miss, then Oladipo came off a ball screen, found an opening and drove to the bucket for a score and a foul, hitting the free throw to tie the game. "I saw two people on Cody and I just drove," Oladipo said. "I felt him on me, and I felt the contact, so I just tried to finish strong. Luckily I got an And-1."

The Rams had a chance to take the lead again, but guard Troy Daniels missed from three. Oladipo grabbed a rebound and Crean opted not to call a timeout. Oladipo took the ball all the way to the rim and was blocked, but that worked brilliantly for Sheehey. "Well, they made a great play guarding the rim," Sheehey said. "And at that time I thought the momentum was on our side. We had made a little comeback there. And I'm comfortable shooting at that range. It was pretty open, so I decided to take it."

Indiana Hoosiers guard Victor Oladipo (4) deflects the inbound pass of Virginia Commonwealth Rams guard Darius Theus (10).

(Right) Head coach Tom Crean gets in Indiana Hoosiers guard Jordan Hulls (1) face at a timeout.

(Far right) Indiana Hoosiers forward Christian Watford (2) celebrates a 3-pointer.

VA. COMMONWEALTH 61

	Min	3PFG	AFG	FT	O-	R	A	PF	Pts
Reddic, f	25	0- 0	4- 8	0- 2	1- 3	0	5		8
Burgess, f	36	4- 9	4-10	3- 5	2- 7	0	2		15
Haley, c	18	0- 0	1- 2	1- 2	1- 3	0	1		3
Theus, g	38	0- 1	1- 3	0- 0	1- 1	5	2	2	2
Daniels, g	28	2- 8	4-13	0- 0	0- 2	0	2		10
Weber	11	0- 0	2- 3	0- 0	1- 1	0	2		4
Brandenbrg	27	2- 7	5-12	1- 2	0- 2	3	1		13
Graham	17	1- 4	2- 6	1- 2	0- 1	0	1		6
team					2- 3				
Totals		9-30	23-57	6-13	8-23	8	16		61
Shooting		.300	.404	.462					

INDIANA 63

	Min	3PFG	AFG	FT	O-	R	A	PF	Pts
Watford, f	28	4- 5	5-10	2- 2	0- 5	1	3		16
Sheehey, f	31	0- 1	4- 6	0- 0	0- 3	4	2		8
Zeller, c	33	0- 0	5- 9	6- 8	4-13	1	1		16
Hulls, g	30	1- 4	2- 7	0- 0	0- 4	1	3		5
Oladipo, g	34	0- 0	4- 5	1- 1	1- 5	6	3		9
Abell	16	0- 1	2- 6	0- 0	1- 2	0	0		4
Pritchard	6	0- 0	1- 1	0- 0	1- 1	0	1		2
Roth	13	1- 1	1- 1	0- 0	0- 0	0	0		3
Elston	9	0- 1	0- 1	0- 0	0- 0	0	0		0
team					1- 3				
Totals		6-13	24-46	9-11	8-36	13	13		63
Shooting		.462	.522	.818					

Virginia Commonwealth (29-7)	42	19—61	
Indiana (27-8)	51	22—63	

Blocks: Virginia Commonwealth 3 (Reddic, Graham, Haley), Indiana 2 (Zeller, Oladipo). **Turnovers:** Virginia Commonwealth 11 (Theus 2, Brandenberg 2, Burgess 2, Weber 2, Haley, Daniels, Reddic), Indiana 22 (Oladipo 5, Hulls 5, Zeller 4, Sheehey 3, Abell 2, Elston 2, Watford). **Steals:** Virginia Commonwealth 10 (Theus 5, Brandenberg 2, Graham, Weber, Daniels), Indiana 6 (Hulls 2, Watford 2, Oladipo, Sheehey). **Officials:** Tom Eades, Mike Littlewood, Tony Padilla.

Indiana Hoosiers forward Cody Zeller (40) attempts a layup.

Indiana Hoosiers forward Will Sheehey (10) dunks the ball .

Indiana Hoosiers guard Victor Oladipo (4) drives the ball around Virginia Commonwealth Rams guard Rob Brandenberg (11).

Virginia Commonwealth Rams center D.J. Haley (33) draws the charge from Indiana Hoosiers forward Cody Zeller (40).

Indiana Hoosiers forward Cody Zeller (40) blocks the shot of Virginia Commonwealth Rams forward Juvonte Reddic (15) as Indiana Hoosiers forward Christian Watford (2) and Indiana Hoosiers guard Victor Oladipo (4) help on defense.

(Left) Indiana Hoosiers guard Victor Oladipo (4) goes for the dunk as Virginia Commonwealth Rams guard/forward Bradford Burgess (20) defends.

(Right) Indiana Hoosiers forward Will Sheehey (10) celebrates the Hoosier win.

(Below) The Hoosier bench celebrates after Indiana Hoosiers forward Will Sheehey (10) hits the game winning bucket.

Indiana Hoosiers forward Cody Zeller (40) wins the tip off during the Indiana Kentucky 2012 NCAA Men's Basketball Sweet Sixteen game at the Georgia Dome in Atlanta, Ga., Friday, March 23, 2012.

Dream Season Comes to Close

Top-seeded Kentucky shoots down Hoosiers in Sweet 16, 102-90

By Dustin Dopirak

With his head firmly tilted toward the floor, Jordan Hulls shuffled all the way to the final seat on Indiana's bench and waited to enter the post-game handshake line until there was no postponing it any further.

It was as if he just wasn't ready for it to end. Really, none of the Hoosiers were.

But on Friday night — really, early Saturday morning — Indiana's magic season of rebirth came to a close against the team the Hoosiers had beaten in December to announce their return to prominence. No. 4 seeded Indiana kept up with No. 1 Kentucky throughout a maniacally paced and brilliantly played NCAA South Regional semifinal at the Georgia Dome, but the Wildcats' length, athleticism and ability to draw fouls was too much in the long run, and they advanced to the Elite Eight with a 102-90 victory in front of a crowd of 24,731 that was largely partisan to their side.

Still, the campaign that ended in Atlanta is one that will long be remembered in Indiana lore. Just four years after the program was decimated and a year after their third straight 20-loss season, the Hoosiers reached the Sweet 16 for the first time since 2002, won 27 games for the first time since the 1992-93 season and defeated three AP top 5 teams in the regular season for the first time in school history.

And in the Hoosiers' final game, they went down swinging as hard as they had all year.

"The Indiana men, and I mean quote me, the Indiana men, mighty men, as I've learned from my brother-in-laws and the way they describe their players, the Indiana mighty men , they gave it all," an emotional coach Tom Crean said in his post-game press conference. "They left it all on that court. I'm proud of what they did."

Said freshman forward Cody Zeller: "It's tough to lose like this. We came in planning to win it. That's why this one really hurts."

The biggest reason they didn't was fouls and what Kentucky did with them. Indiana outshot Kentucky, making 36 of 69 field goals (52.2 percent) compared to the Wildcats 31-for-64 performance (48.4 percent). However, Kentucky went to the line 37 times and hit 35.

Crean hinted he thought the free throw differential was a tad unfair. "When they make 22 more free throws and take 20 more, I don't know if I could've imagined that," Crean said. "I wouldn't have imagined a game like this having a free throw discrepancy of 20. It is what it is. We did a lot of good things. They shot 20 more free throws. That's the game."

How much of that was officiating and how much of that was simply Kentucky's length and strength inside is difficult to tell. The Wildcats were often able to break the Hoosiers down off the dribble and draw fouls deep in the paint.

"They're great drivers," Zeller said. "They were attacking pretty hard throughout the game. Late in the game they had to foul just to try to close the margin a little bit. But they got to the bonus pretty early, and that really helped them out pretty well."

Both teams got five players in double figures. Freshman forward Michael Kidd-Gilchrist led Kentucky with 24 points and 10 rebounds. Sophomore guard Doron Lamb had 21, and senior forward Darius Miller had 19. Freshman point guard Marquis Teague had 14 points and seven assists, while sophomore forward Terrence Jones had 12 points.

Indiana junior forward Christian Watford led all scorers with 27 points. Zeller had 20, sophomore guard Victor Oladipo had 15 points and three assists, while junior guard Jordan Hulls had 12 points and nine assists. Sophomore Will Sheehey added 10, but he and Oladipo both fouled out as the Hoosiers had to deal with foul trouble for most of the evening.

In the first half, the Hoosiers were able to take advantage of Kentucky freshman forward Anthony Davis's foul trouble and trailed just 50-47 in a shot-for-shot first half. However, the Wildcats took control early in the second half, thanks in large part to two 3-pointers by Miller that gave Kentucky an eight-point lead. The Hoosiers kept rallying back and cut the deficit to four, but the Wildcats were always able to keep them at an arm's length.

"We made a couple of personnel mistakes," Crean said. "There were a couple of times that they got to their strengths. Jones got to his strengths, Miller got to his strengths. ... We broke down a little bit. But you know, we were able to come back and get some of that, but they got momentum and we were always playing uphill from that point on. We were hanging right there. We had some guys running on fumes. I said to John (Calipari), make sure you've got enough energy to win this game. That game took a lot out of everybody, no question about it."

The Hoosiers cut the deficit to 82-77 with 5:14 left and 86-79 with 3:24 to go, but Kentucky made all 16 free throws they made from that point forward. That caused Indiana's season to end before the Hoosiers wanted to, but not before this team brought the program back.

Indiana Hoosiers forward Christian Watford (2) shoots over Kentucky Wildcats forward Terrence Jones (3).

INDIANA 90

	Min	3PFG	AFG	FT	O- R	A	PF	Pts
Watford, f	36	3-9	9-20	6-8	0-5	2	4	27
Sheehey, f	35	0-1	5-8	0-0	2-4	0	5	10
Zeller, c	27	0-0	9-14	2-2	3-7	2	3	20
Hulls, g	32	2-4	5-12	0-0	1-3	9	3	12
Oladipo, g	20	0-1	6-8	3-4	0-2	3	5	15
Moore	1	0-0	0-0	0-0	0-0	0	2	0
Abell	14	0-1	2-3	2-2	0-1	0	2	6
Pritchard	13	0-0	0-2	0-0	3-3	0	2	0
Roth	14	0-2	0-2	0-0	0-0	0	0	0
Elston	8	0-0	0-0	0-0	1-0	3	0	1	0
team					2- 3			
Totals		5-18	36-69	13-17	12-31	16	27	90
Shooting		.278	.522	.765				

KENTUCKY 102

	Min	3PFG	AFG	FT	O- R	A	PF	Pts
Jones, f	27	1-2	5-9	1-2	3-5	0	3	12
K-Glchrst, f	34	0-1	7-15	10-10	6-10	1	2	24
Davis, c	25	0-1	2-5	5-6	2-12	2	2	9
Lamb, g	38	1-1	6-10	8-8	0-3	2	2	21
Teague, g	36	0-2	4-14	6-6	0-3	7	3	14
Miller	31	2-2	6-8	5-5	2-3	0	4	19
Beckham	1	0-0	0-0	0-0	0-0	0	0	0
Vargas	2	0-0	0-1	0-0	1-1	0	1	0
Wiltjer	6	1-1	1-2	0-0	0-0	0	1	3
team					1- 2			
Totals		5-10	31-64	35-37	15-39	12	18	102
Shooting		.500	.484	.946				

(Above left) Kentucky Wildcats guard Marquis Teague (25) defends the dunk attempt of Indiana Hoosiers forward Tom Pritchard (25).

(Right) Indiana Hoosiers guard Victor Oladipo (4) lays the ball in around Kentucky Wildcats forward Anthony Davis (23).

Indiana (27-9)	47	43 —	90
Kentucky (34-2)	50	52 —	102

Blocks: Indiana 2 (Watford 2), Kentucky 4 (Davis 3, Jones). **Turnovers:** Indiana 8 (Zeller 3, Abell 2, Oladipo, Watford, Sheehey), Kentucky 6 (Kidd-Gilchrist 2, Teague 2, Jones, Lamb). **Steals:** Indiana 3 (Hulls, Sheehey, Watford), Kentucky 3 (Jones, Teague, Lamb).
Officials: Mark Whitehead, Ed Corbett, Ray Natili. **A:** 24,731.

(Above) Indiana Hoosiers guard Victor Oladipo (4) fouls Kentucky Wildcats forward Terrence Jones (3).

(Right) Indiana Hoosiers forward Will Sheehey (10) tries laying the ball in around Kentucky Wildcats forward Anthony Davis (23).

Head coach Tom Crean takes a timeout and gets in the face of his team.

Head coach Tom Crean gets his team pumped up on the sideline to get them to get a stop with less than 30 seconds left in the half.

Indiana Hoosiers forward Christian Watford (2) hangs his head at the Indiana bench after the game.

Indiana Hoosiers forward Cody Zeller (40) and Indiana Hoosiers guard Matt Roth (30) fight back the tears after the Indiana Kentucky 2012 NCAA Men's Basketball Sweet Sixteen game.

Indiana Hoosiers guard Jordan Hulls (1) and Indiana Hoosiers guard Verdell Jones III (12) wait for interviews to conclude in the locker room.

Hulls Taking Charge

Tired of losing, former Bloomington South star decides to take over as IU team leader

By Dustin Dopirak

Verdell Jones III will remember the spring and summer of 2011 as the offseason when Jordan Hulls snapped. Before that, Hulls was the quiet, scrappy little hometown fan favorite who kept his mouth shut, passed the ball and made 3-pointers and free throws. The Bloomington South graduate spent every free moment in Assembly Hall or Cook Hall, and hoped his Indiana teammates would take notice and follow.

But he didn't demand it.

This summer, though, after suffering through 41 losses in his first two seasons as a college basketball player, Hulls reached two critical junctures in his mind. He found the confidence to lead and decided he could no longer stand defeat.

Teammates relay stories of this new Hulls barking orders, hollering at teammates and even kicking them out of strength and conditioning sessions or open gyms for sloppy performance. It's not easy to picture the baby-faced 6-footer screaming at his much bigger and older-looking colleagues, but there isn't a witness who denies the stories.

He's acting like a captain.

"It was funny because he'd been so quiet," said Jones, a senior guard who also is considered among the squad's leaders. "All the sudden, he just snaps. And we're like, 'What's going on?'"

Said Hulls: "I guess I did kind of snap, because I'm sick of losing. I think everybody's sick of losing. Somebody needed to step up and say something about it. I totally embraced that role."

And that's exactly what Tom Crean was waiting for.

The fourth-year coach always wanted Hulls to serve as a model for the program he's had to build back from the rubble of the Kelvin Sampson scandal and the roster purge that followed. He needed someone on the floor that teams could look to in critical junctions in games, because too often in the first three years, it has fallen to Crean to direct traffic in those situations. It would also help if Hulls could become the face of a program trying to rediscover its roots.

Because Hulls is, perhaps, the living embodiment of the principles of Indiana basketball, not just at IU but the entire state. He's a self-made player who has dedicated almost all the time he's able to stand to advancing beyond the limits of his size, speed and athleticism. By earning a state championship, the Indiana Mr. Basketball award, and a scholarship and a starting job at what is arguably still the state's flagship basketball program, he's already proven the power of Hoosier ideals like fundamentals and team basketball.

"Not being from Indiana, I did have a certain kind of mold that I thought an Indiana basketball player would fill," sophomore swingman Will Sheehey said. "And I'm pretty sure he was it."

Now he's taken it upon himself to make sure the rest of the Hoosiers fill it too.

The Ultimate Hoosier

One of the first things you see when you enter the Hulls household on Bloomington's south side is a framed picture of the tiny basketball court in Knightstown where much of the movie "Hoosiers" was filmed.

It's a memento Hulls earned in 2009 for participating in the Hoosier Reunion Classic, a six-year-old all-star game played in the old gym as an homage to the movie. It's signed by the man who wrote the screenplay to the film, a family friend and rabid Indiana fan: "To Jordan, From one Hoosier to another, Angelo Pizzo."

It couldn't be more appropriate.

"The only thing I really knew about Indiana basketball was the movie 'Hoosiers,'" senior guard Verdell Jones III said. "So if you look at Jordy and you look at the characters on Hoosiers, there's a direct correlation. He's very fundamental, can shoot it. I think he's the perfect prototype for Indiana basketball."

But really, Hulls fits the Indiana archetype even better than the characters in the 1986 film. Which of the Hickory Huskers made more out of less? Which of them was as good as Hulls at making his teammates better as a pass-first point guard?

None of them. Not even Jimmy Chitwood. Even the movie's creator wouldn't dispute that.

"Maybe it's my own bias, but there is a certain aesthetic about how the game should be played," Pizzo said. "Really, it's a combination of the classic Steve Alford, Jimmy Chitwood, Larry Bird, Rick Mount — guys who just are dead-eye shooters. The next level up from that is the unselfish player. The guy that can make that pass. Take what the team will get him. It's part of understanding how all the components work together, understanding that there is no glory to personal numbers. It's only in the team's wins."

That's how Hulls was taught to play, and as it was with so many Indiana kids, it started at the very beginning.

'It's just part of me'

"Jordan's probably 2 or 3 years old, and he's just got the basketball and he's just dribbling around everywhere at his older brother's games," said Hulls' father J.C. "It was kind of comical. You see this little blonde-headed, two-foot high kid. The ball was just as big as him. And I don't know why. That just made sense to him. Basketball was just what he did."

Hulls was coached intensely in the fundamentals by J.C., who played at Vincennes Junior College, and his grandfather, John, a high school friend of Bob Knight's in Orrville, Ohio, who went on to work as his assistant at Army and then at Indiana in Knight's first two years there.

Jordan started on ball-handling drills at the age of 5, doing cone drills and working with Pete Maravich instructional videos. He spent every free moment of the summers in fifth and sixth grade working on his left hand and recreating his jumper once he became strong enough to shoot from the shoulder and not the hip. Spending time in the gym became an obsession for Hulls, and it still is.

"It's just something my dad instilled in me, that work ethic," Hulls said. "Just trying to get better. It's just something I've always done, I don't know. It's just part of me, I guess. It's kind of hard for me to leave the gym. I hate not being the last guy to leave the gym."

J.C. made it clear — he admits, to a fault — that Hulls use those skills for the good of the team, and that it should be more important to him to move the ball than to look for his own shot.

"As he came up, I said, 'You run the show as the point guard,'" J.C. said. "I don't care if you score. I don't care. If you're open, shoot. But I just want you to get the ball with the guy that's open and get it to him at the right spacing, in the right spot.'"

Hulls was always good at that, and that was the reason he won everywhere he went even as the competition got taller and more athletic, and he stayed at 6-feet tall and about a half-step slow in lateral quickness.

As a high schooler, he lost just seven times in a combined four years on junior varsity and varsity. His career culminated with the undefeated 2008-09 South squad that won the Class 4A state title and finished with a No. 3 overall national ranking.

"He hates to lose," South coach J.R. Holmes said. "Hates more than anything in the world to lose. Whether he scores zero points or two

points or 20 points. I really believe he does not care. The only thing he cares about, he wants to win. And when given that opportunity on your team, he does whatever it takes to win. If it's shooting. If it's passing, diving in the stands, give up your body for loose balls. You see some prima donna players never get on the floor. He's gonna do that. He hates to lose."

His teammates knew that, because he'd proven it time and again since grade school. So when he was put in leadership roles, he didn't have to say much for them to listen.

"In high school, he wasn't real vocal, but the players knew when he was serious," Holmes said. "He wasn't trying to scream loud and try to put on a show. Look at me, 'YOU GUYS!' It was, 'Hey, no. Let's get this going.' It was a quiet, calm situation."

But leading in college required more.

The Right Time

Going back to high school, Hulls had a sense of his place in the program. He played point guard as a sophomore, but never felt completely comfortable trying to be vocal, always hoping that teammates would see his work ethic and copy it. As a junior, he was slightly more comfortable but still looked at that South squad as then senior guard Tanner Blackwell's team. It wasn't until his senior year that he felt comfortable taking over.

So it wasn't very surprising then, that Hulls' first instinct when he went to Indiana was to defer. There were two older ball-handlers on the squad in Jones and Jeremiah Rivers, plus then-senior Devan Dumes.

Crean and assistant coach Tim Buckley especially wanted Hulls to be more vocal immediately. They told him so, and they told his father as well. They all struggled to get that through to him but came to realize that it wouldn't happen until Hulls was ready.

"They would come to me and say, 'Well what do we need to do?'"

J.C. said. "I said, 'Hey, I'm telling him. You're telling him.' But I remember I had a chat with (former IU basketball player) Chris Reynolds and (former IU football star) Anthony Thompson about leadership. You know, here's two guys that were leaders of their team at IU. I said, 'Am I missing something here? There's no question he's got it in him. I know he can do it.' Both of them told me, 'He will know when it's time. And you can't push him into that.'"

Before Hulls could know when it was time, he had to believe he was worthy. After his freshman year, he still believed he had too much work to do on his game to command respect. He scored 6.4 points per game that season, but felt like his game was too limited and spent most of the following summer in the gym by himself trying to change that.

Sophomore year allowed him to make a big step, because it forced him to be more aggressive in games. Injuries to Verdell Jones III and Christian Watford in January forced him to be the Hoosiers' top offensive option and to look for opportunities to shoot instead of always passing. It was, for that stretch, more his team than anyone else's. He finished the year third in scoring behind Jones and Watford with 11.0 points per game and led the squad with 94 assists. By just about every measure, he was the Hoosiers' most efficient offensive player.

Hulls also began to speak out more — but not enough. This new voice still didn't satisfy the coaching staff and it didn't do enough to stop the losing either. The Hoosiers followed a 10-21 season in 2009-10 by going 12-20 last season.

So his father made one more plea, just before Hulls left for an exhibition tour in China with Victor Oladipo and a team called Reach USA.

"I said, 'Let me just tell you,'" J.C. said. "'If you don't change, you got two years left. If you don't change what you're doing in practices and workouts, I can pretty well tell ya, it won't be any different than

your first two years. You know what needs to be done. Now, you gotta share it, and you gotta pull those guys along.'"

When he got back from China, that's exactly what he started doing. Open gym workouts, by several accounts, became his domain, and he was barking at teammates right alongside strength and conditioning coach Je'Ney Jackson. Things didn't change once practice started.

"Right now, Jordy's kind of like the floor manager," junior forward Derek Elston said. "We'll go red and white every day. If you're on Jordy's team, he'll tell you exactly what to do. There is no ifs, ands or buts. If you have a question, you go to Jordy now."

Said Hulls: "It was a learning process for me. I was trying to learn what it takes, what I need to do."

So now the Hoosiers respect him and know they can rely on him. The next step, Crean said, is to revere him deeply enough that they almost fear him.

That he isn't big enough to physically intimidate doesn't matter. Travis Diener isn't much bigger than Hulls at 6-1, 175 pounds, but Crean said that at Marquette, Diener was the one player on the squad who could bring Dwyane Wade to tears.

And he has to be able to command that respect in games. It's one thing to get in teammates' faces in practice. It's something else to do it when the lights are on, the clock is ticking and the score is close.

"They've gotta respond to what he says, right now," Crean said. "It's not, 'Well, Jordan will take care of it.' It's not, well, 'Jordan won't get in my face.' It's not well, 'Jordan's a good guy, and we'll go to the mall afterwards, but if I don't listen to him right now, no big deal.' No. But he's putting a little more challenge out there."

Because now that Hulls has snapped, he doesn't want to lose anymore.

A Job Well Done for Verdell Jones III

Senior guard has played a big part in IU's resurgence

By Dustin Dopirak

Verdell Jones III is at peace.

The Indiana senior guard is in a situation he's never been entirely comfortable with, surrounded by reporters trying to probe him about his innermost thoughts. He's toed a fine line with the media in his four years in Bloomington, providing enough honesty to be accommodating but being sure to maintain something of an emotional wall.

But in this case, the still baby-faced Jones exudes an easy serenity, smiling and laughing with the hood of his bluish sweatshirt hanging sideways off his right shoulder. He draws guffaws from the reporters with stories from conditioning sessions in his freshman year and self-deprecates about the twiggy frame he came to Bloomington with. He is as relaxed in the presence of microphones as he's ever been.

Part of that is just the mood around the entire Assembly Hall/Cook Hall compound following IU's landmark upset of No. 5 Michigan State. But more of it is that with Jones' career coming to a close, he finally knows validation.

More than any other member of this graduating senior class, Jones had the opportunity to avoid the wreckage that was the Indiana basketball program circa spring 2008. And more than any of the other four, he has been, for better and worse, the face of a painful rebuild, suffering the slings and arrows that come with such a position. He's been through 73 losses and had to answer publicly for most of them, and he knows full well that his lofty standing among IU's all-time leading scorers — he's 23rd with 1,340 points — will be eternally derided because they coincided with all of those defeats.

But he also knows that a week from today, he will see the name "Indiana" back in an NCAA Tournament bracket. That means he accomplished what he set out to do, and that all the pain was worth it.

"It's been a great four years," Jones said. "It's something that,

could I have gone somewhere else? Yes. Do I regret coming here? Not at all. Not one bit. These four years have shaped me as a man."

Staying Committed

Unlike fellow seniors Matt Roth and Tom Pritchard, both of whom had committed to Kelvin Sampson before the former coach was forced to resign in the wake of NCAA recruiting violations, Jones had an idea what he was getting into when he committed. He had offers from Minnesota and Billy Gillespie's Kentucky squad in the spring of his senior year, when he was one of the highest-rated point guards still unsigned. He didn't know quite how decimated the roster would be when he arrived, but he knew it was going to be bad and kept his commitment even as it kept getting worse.

"When I first committed a lot of the old guys were still here,"

Jones said. "Then after I signed my letter of intent, it seemed like each day, a new guy left and another guy left, so it just started crumbling. I really wanted to stay, because if you're a part of the group that helps rebuild something like this, you'll be remembered forever as the foundation. I saw what coach Crean was seeing, and I just believed in the same thing he believed in, and I thought we could turn it around."

Said Jones father, Verdell Jones Jr.: "We knew it was not the best of situations going in, but still, it was Indiana. We accepted all of that. We've never taught our boys to quit at anything, and we realized that even through tough times and adversity, what doesn't kill you makes you stronger."

The elder Jones works in truancy and student advocacy with Champaign (Ill.) Unit 4 Schools, runs a basketball skill development and leadership academy and is profoundly religious. He raised his son up with plenty of adages and proverbs about withstanding adversity and building character. His son needed just about all of them to keep his head through the last three years.

The 2008-09 campaign was brutal on everybody, as the 6-25

mark was worse than anything Indiana had ever seen. But the spindly Jones, who arrived at Bloomington at 6-foot-5 and just 165 pounds, was considered one of the team's bright spots, averaging 11.0 points per game and closing the season with back-to-back 23-point games.

But Jones felt more of the burden personally for the next two seasons. In both cases he was the team's top perimeter scorer, and so much of the Hoosiers' fortunes rode on whether or not he was being effective. He led the team with 14.9 points per game as a sophomore and scored 12.5 as a junior, but he caught heat for his decision-making — 170 turnovers in 59 games in those two seasons — and sometimes forcing shots that weren't there. Some of that heat came from the more impatient sects of the Indiana fan base, but a lot of it came from himself, because he believed that the Hoosiers could and should be better than the 10-21 and 12-20 marks they posted.

"He, at times, had a sense of frustration because he wanted so desperately to bring a winner for the families of the guys he played with," Jones Jr. said. "For the legacy of the program and so forth and so on. There were times that he was frustrated because it wasn't necessarily happening as quick. When it became tougher is when you could really see the light at the end of the tunnel and you realized it wasn't Amtrak."

But in his ups and downs, Jones said he found something of a personal affirmation. His father said that an integral part of his son's character is his ability to stay composed, and Jones continued to prove that to himself.

"It's taught me that I'm a very strong person mentally," Jones said. "I don't get caught up in the highs and I don't get caught up in the lows. When we're doing well I enjoy it, but I don't let it get to me. When I'm playing well I don't let it get to me, because I know the next day I could have zero points, and the fans are booing me. And when that happens, it only takes one good game and now they're cheering your name. I'm just a mentally strong person, and I think these four years have made me more mentally strong."

The Payoff

There may not be a better indicator of Jones' maturity this season than this. He heads into tonight's game with 23 more assists (92) this season than made field goals (69).

There is a caricature on the internet chat boards of Jones as a selfish player, but those numbers prove that to be empirically false. Without prompting from Crean, he came into the season with the understanding that the primary offensive burden wasn't going to be his anymore, and that he could best serve the team by moving the basketball.

This team was going to be better than any he'd played with before. He could tell that in preseason, and the best way he could make sure that finally translated into victories would be to put his teammates in better positions to be successful.

"We have a lot of explosive offensive talent between Christian (Watford) and Victor (Oladipo), Cody (Zeller), Jordan (Hulls), the list keeps going on," Jones said. "I don't need to go out and and shoot 10-15 shots a game like I may have freshman and sophomore year. … I've taken more of the role of trying to get those guys going before I get going. Because once they get going, no one can stop us."

And while he hasn't been shooting as much, he's picked up his game in other areas, becoming a better defender and rebounder and a much more vocal leader. He forms a two-headed captaincy with junior point guard Jordan Hulls, who delivers instructions, and Jones makes sure they are obeyed.

"He's a great reminder," Crean said. "Which I think is what leadership is a lot of times anyway. He reminds guys of what they have to do. He reinforces it. Verdell has learned that you can impact winning a lot of different ways."

And after three years of suffering, that's helped him finally learn what winning feels like. And he's basked in the contrast of the joy of this season against the pain of the rest of his career. And he's awaiting the defining moment next week when, one way or the other, the Hoosiers will receive an NCAA Tournament berth.

"It's a feeling I've been waiting for since freshman year," Jones said. "Assistant coach (Bennie) Seltzer always talks about the feeling that he had when he was at Oklahoma, at Marquette, how great a feeling that is to be watching TV and knowing that your name is going to be called soon. Not to be on the bubble, but knowing that your name is going to be called. I can't wait for that day, I'm gonna cherish it."

Sheehey, Oladipo Bring Own Brand of Energy to IU

By Dustin Dopirak

If someone on the team was ever going to be inflamed enough by an opponent's press-conference quote to call that player out on it, the Indiana Hoosiers knew it would be Will Sheehey. And there he was on Thursday night, wearing a stone-cold expression that belied the fact that the Hoosiers had just won their first NCAA Tournament game, calling out New Mexico State's Wendell McKines.

"He said some things in the press conference earlier that were a little questionable," Sheehey said after IU's 79-66 win on Thursday. "So we took it upon ourselves that he didn't get those touches. He said something about no mammal can guard him or something like that. So I guess Victor (Oladipo) is not human."

Injured senior guard Verdell Jones III just laughed when he heard that one.

"He told me after he said it, I was like 'Oh, Lord, you're gonna get us all in trouble,'" Jones said. "That's just Will for you. If you knew Will at all, you wouldn't be surprised if he said that."

And then on the opposite end of the spectrum is Oladipo, Sheehey's perpetually smiling classmate and fellow swingman, who tends to let those and most other slights roll off his back. The one who is singing a song wherever he goes and is so good at that that Indiana brought him out to sing Usher's "U Got It Bad," at Hoosier Hysteria in October.

They are polar opposites but extremely close friends. In a sense — entirely unrelated to the fact that Oladipo is black and Sheehey is white — they have brought something of a yin and yang relationship to Indiana which has altered the attitude of the program in their two years. Oladipo's engaging and upbeat spirit and showmanship and Sheehey's sometimes dark ferocity are a big part of what has inspired the Hoosiers to go from 28-66 in coach Tom Crean's first three seasons to their current spot in the Round of 32.

"Opposites attract," Oladipo said, "but he's my partner in crime."

Said Crean: "They came at a time when guys were kind of at the crossroads. How much do they love it. We're not winning, all this hard work, all this stuff that I'm asking them to do and we're doing, and we're not getting a payoff for it, and these guys really brought another level of energy to the program."

They both came to Indiana as outsiders with Sheehey from Stuart, Fla., and Oladipo from the Maryland suburbs of Washington, D.C. That isn't always easy in a state that takes enormous provincial pride in its high school basketball and prefers the players at its flagship institution to be homegrown. They also came in unheralded as three-star recruits with Sheehey, rated the No. 141 player in the Class of 2010 and Oladipo No. 144.

"I don't think we had any fanfare to be honest with you," Sheehey said. "Not being from Indiana and not being in the top 10 recruiting class or whatever. It didn't really help our cause, but we just go out and try to play hard and do what the team needs to win." But they were determined to prove any and all doubters wrong. To do that together, they relied on their similarities, most notably a determined work ethic both on the floor and off, where both are accomplished students. Junior point guard Jordan Hulls may the Hoosiers' most devout gym rat, but Sheehey and Oladipo were right behind him, using the newly minted Cook Hall at all available hours.

"I remember just first coming in with Will, and the first thing we did was go to the gym," Oladipo said. "I could tell just from that that he was in it to win it just like me."

The Hoosiers didn't win immediately with Oladipo and Sheehey in the fold last season, but it was evident they would serve as catalysts in a chain reaction that would lead to Indiana's rebuild. Native sons or not, they quickly endeared themselves to the fan base with high-light reel dunks and athleticism and relentless energy. That became infectious to the rest of the group, both because it was inspiring and because teammates knew they had to follow their lead or be left behind.

It was even more of a driving force this offseason than it was during last year, and it was evident in the physical and skill development of many of their teammates that Sheehey and Oladipo had pushed the squad a step further.

"We had a lot more guys that had a hard work, work ethic, gym rat mentality that spring, summer and fall than we had in the past," Crean said. "And some guys changed, but I also think there was, 'We've got to keep up, this is going to be really, really competitive.' And Will and Victor led the way."

Once the team returned to the games, they led in different ways. Oladipo was the demonstrative one, flashing his "Know Us" sign by pointing to his eyes after dunks and big plays and rousing the Assembly Hall crowd at home games. Sheehey is less vocal, but there's an orneriness to him that makes him a big part of the team's backbone. When Christian Watford took a hard foul at the end of a January win over Penn State, Sheehey popped off the bench and was jawing with a Penn State player before drawing an ejection. "He can be ruthless sometimes," Hulls said. "He doesn't like

to put up with anything, if he doesn't like it, he'll let you know about it. He just kind of speaks his mind, but that's the way Will is. But that's why we love Will. He brings that fierceness to us."

Their games are less different than their personalities. They can both defend positions 1-5 if necessary, and they can both go to the rim. Oladipo's more explosive off the dribble-drive, Sheehey is a better shooter, but they both bring the athleticism that allows the Hoosiers to be an up-tempo team.

"They add a piece to the puzzle that most of us don't have," Jones said. "That athleticism and that high-motor energy. They're great talents."

And despite their differences, they've combined to be the soul of Indiana's rebuild.

Watford's Eyes a Window Into His Game

By Dustin Dopirak

Kory Barnett can tell by the look in Christian Watford's eyes. Barnett's official title with the Indiana basketball program is senior guard, and the walk-on seldom gets on the court in that role, but his greater value is behind the scenes where he's really a coach-in-training. He takes the temperature of the locker room before every game, looking for signs that might reveal who's in the right frame of mind and who isn't.

To know if the Hoosiers are going to get the Watford they want, Barnett said, he has to look closely — past the junior forward's slow, swaggering gait and easy-like-Sunday-morning demeanor and into the places where he can tell if the fire is burning.

"Every player has his edge," Barnett said. "Christian's edge is not to the point where he's in the locker room cussing, pushing guys around and getting ready. His edge is a quietness, almost a calmness, like the calmness before the storm. He sits in that locker room, and you can kind of look in his eyes, and you can tell that he's ready a lot of the times. There's times when he's not. Every player has games when they're not, but when Christian's ready, you can tell. When he comes out and he plays, I think it overflows to the rest of the team where it brings everyone else's edge to a whole other level."

That's what happened last week against Illinois when Watford's two-handed dunk on Meyers Leonard brought the bench to its feet. That's what happened when he blew up for 25 points against Michigan back on Jan. 5. And of course, that's what happened in December against Kentucky when he hit the shot that earned him an immortal place in Indiana basketball lore.

But as Barnett said, there are times when that edge isn't there. Times when there's a complacency or a listlessness to Watford's game that renders the team's most versatile skill set ineffective and forces the Hoosiers to look elsewhere for scoring, rebounding, defense and energy. Losses to Minnesota, Nebraska and Michigan, in which he shot a combined 7-for-22 and averaged 6.7 points, spring to mind.

"I've been on him all his life about playing hard all the time," Watford's father, Ernest, said. ". He has to play with a lot of effort and a lot of momentum. I think sometimes during the course of a game that slips a little bit."

As this resurgent Indiana team heads toward its first postseason since 2008, that's what makes Watford the Hoosiers' biggest variable. He is the player with the greatest distance between his ceiling and his floor, and therefore the X-factor that can add or subtract the most from IU's ability to make a deep NCAA Tournament run.

At his best, he's Indiana's second-best player and most difficult matchup as a 6-foot-9, 225-pound forward who can step out and hit 3-pointers with regularity, attack off the dribble, score in the post, and defend any position on the floor. At his worst, he can virtually disappear.

Said junior guard Jordan Hulls: "Christian can be as great as he wants to be, whenever he puts his mind to it."

Putting in the Work

Watford's was never a case of a sense of entitlement or lack of work ethic. Ernest Watford would never allow that.

Ernest was himself a high school basketball star and played at Southern Junior College in Birmingham, Ala. As a player he was almost entirely self-made. He lost his father to a heart illness when he was 13 years old. His older brothers didn't play much, and his mother was working at a dry cleaner to support the family. He had general role models for life, but no one to give him the road map to a Division I basketball scholarship.

So he vowed from the beginning to do that for Christian.

"I didn't have a mentor with me," the elder Watford said. "So I've tried to do that for my son. I wasn't going to allow him to think he was something that he wasn't. I was all-county and all-state and all that kind of stuff, but I realized at the end of the day that I wasn't all that I thought I was. Learning from that, when I had my son I wanted to make sure know that he knew he had to work all the time."

From first through eighth grade, Ernest coached Christian's teams at his private school, carving out hours in the gym while also serving as a Jefferson County sheriff's deputy. When Christian was in about fourth grade, they ratcheted up his individual workouts outside of practice, focusing on developing perimeter skills. Ernest knew Christian would be tall — Ernest is 6-5, and his wife Belinda, who works at a Birmingham high school is 5-9 — but not so tall that he wouldn't have to play outside the paint.

"He wanted to instill in me that I wasn't going to grow to be 7-foot," Christian said. "The way the game of basketball was changing, you had to be able to put the ball on the floor and had to be able to shoot the basketball. When I was young, even when I was the biggest guy on the floor, my dad made sure that I was out on the perimeter handling the ball and stuff like that. That kind of rubbed off on me. We just kept working, kept working perimeter skills and perimeter skills, because once you get the outside, you can always get the inside."

sure, it's almost like he was a 6-7 point guard," said Shades Valley coach Mike Burrus, who also called Watford a true gym rat. "You don't find that very often. His skill level was so much higher than anyone else on the team."

There was only one problem with that, though. Watford wasn't quite prepared for the time when that would no longer be the case.

Not So Easy

Even when Christian was still dominating Alabama high school basketball, Ernest noticed a concerning habit in his son that tended to manifest when Shades Valley was up big.

As hard as he was working outside of games, he was sometimes just a little too casual in them.

"I think high school came easy to him," Ernest said. "His skill set was above a lot of kids in the area. He didn't have to play as hard. ... We had that conversation. No doubt we had it. 'At the next level, you will not be able to dominate so easily.'"

When he got to Indiana, that became very clear to him very fast, especially when he had to play power forward as a freshman on a size-challenged team without another post scoring threat.

"Down here, he just shot over everybody," Burrus said. "He was the biggest kid on the block and never had to get in there and bang, I talked to him after the Wisconsin game his freshman year. He said, 'Coach, those dudes are bangers. Everybody they have is just beating the crap out of you the whole game.'"

It was a transition that neither mind nor body were ready for. He was listed at 215 pounds then, but that was admittedly generous. And quite simply, Watford never had an inner desire to beat the crap out of people.

He isn't timid or lazy, but he is eternally mellow. He carries himself with an unshakeable cool, and most of the time, that's a good thing. "There's not much that gets under his skin," teammate Barnett said. "There's always articles. Fans say certain things about our players. A lot of guys, you'll see them get an edge from it. He's just kind of like, 'People are gonna be people. People are gonna say what they want. It's not gonna get to me. I'm gonna play my game.' That's definitely a quality a lot of people don't have that is definitely a positive."

But inside play requires a certain amount of grit and nastiness. Maybe not the same amount that it takes to play linebacker, but still more than Watford produces naturally.

"He's laid back, and sometimes he's too laid back," Watford's father said. "He has to play with emotion, and a lot of times, he doesn't play with enough of it. When he has a quiet night, a lot of times I think he could've got four more defensive stops and six more rebounds just from not settling and not being too laid back."

Changing that has been the goal shared by Watford, his father, Indiana coach Tom Crean and his teammates. Whenever Christian is home or Ernest is in Bloomington, Ernest pulls out the game tape and shows him the plays where he didn't show enough fire and the result of those plays. Crean, who has frequently said that Watford improves at a faster rate when he's locked in than any player he's ever coached, employs similar tactics.

The progress has been steady, although his numbers haven't been on a straight incline. Even as he was being worn out as a freshman by the physical play, he still averaged 12.0 points and 6.0 rebounds

Christian bought into his father's teaching completely. Ernest once tested him to see exactly how self-driven his son was, giving Christian a workout to complete on his own as he left the gym. Ernest returned but watched his son for 45 minutes from outside of his field of vision.

"The kid was working his butt off," Ernest said. "He was working just like I was standing over him. They say character is doing what you're supposed to be doing when people aren't looking at you. That showed me that he wanted to be the best."

At Shades Valley High School, Christian pretty much was. He averaged 22 points and 14 rebounds as a junior, then 25 points and 13 rebounds as a senior to lead the school to a 26-6 mark and was the No. 34 rated player in the Class of 2009, according to Rivals.com. "At his height, with his ability to handle the ball and handle presto make the Big Ten's All-Freshman team. Last season he led the Hoosiers with 16.0 points per game while playing every position from small forward to center for a team that still had little in the post.

The addition of freshman center Cody Zeller has allowed Watford to spend more time on the perimeter this year, and his 37 3-pointers put him second on the team next to Jordan Hulls. However, he's still grabbing 5.5 rebounds per game to go with his 12.3 points and he's become more consistent with his defense and rebounding on nights when he isn't scoring.

"At first I was a guy that had to be driven off of offense more than anything," Watford said. "I had to see the ball go through the basket and stuff like that, but you just grow. That's just all part of growing up. You realize the game of basketball isn't really like that. You have to play defense and keep it going."

One example was Indiana's 78-61 win at Purdue on Feb. 4. Watford went 0-for-7 from the field and finished with just four points but grabbed six rebounds and was key in holding the Boilermakers to 29.6 percent shooting, including a 4-for-14 outing by star forward Robbie Hummel.

"He's gotta continue to understand that your real value comes to the team when you win and how many different ways can you impact winning," Crean said. ". Purdue's a great example. The ball didn't go in the basket, but we don't win the game without him because of the job he did defensively. Because of the job he did on the backboards, because of his will, his intensity."

That's what Barnett sees in Watford's eyes on the nights he's locked in, and what can make him more constant than variable.

Zeller Makes Most of Putting on Freshman 15

By Dustin Dopirak

Take 15 pounds and spread it over a 6-foot-11 body, and you're only talking about a few ounces per inch. The difference between a 215-pound man and a 230-pound man of that height can be noticeable, but only if that man happens to wear tank tops as a standard practice.

When trying to explain the difference between where this Indiana team was expected to finish and where it is, that's where the conversation starts. With the 15 pounds of muscle Cody Zeller put on his 6-11 frame from the time he arrived in Bloomington last May until the season started in November.

To say the freshman forward from Washington is the only reason the Hoosiers morphed from a 12-20 squad last season to the 27-8 team that's currently preparing for its first Sweet 16 game since 2002 is to grossly undervalue the contributions of so many of his teammates, and for that matter, his coach.

But Zeller's gains in weight and strength may have been the most important development of this season, simply because it made all the rest of the pieces fit. Going from 215 to 230 allowed Zeller to play center instead of power forward, where many expected him to play, which allowed the Hoosiers to put five scorers on the floor and allow everyone to play roles that made sense.

"Here in the past, me and Tom (Pritchard) have been playing the five and (it's) kind of out of character for me, especially," junior forward Derek Elston said. "Having Cody down there just kind of opens up everybody's game and lets everybody play their natural position."

The long-term goal was always for Zeller to be the center, but he always had a skinny frame, and the presumption was that it would take a full-year of weight training for him to truly bulk up from 215 pounds. Indiana coach Tom Crean was plenty comfortable using him as a power forward because he had the ball-handling and guard skills for the position, and often used comparisons to former Marquette star Steve Novak when discussing him. Pritchard, a senior, was expected to take some of the beating down low and defend some of the Big Ten's bigger bodies.

But Zeller knew he could put on the necessary size at some point. His older brother Tyler had entered North Carolina at 215 pounds and is now listed on the UNC website at 250.

"He knew that he could do it from his brother," said freshman guard Austin Etherington, Zeller's roommate and former teammate with the Indiana Elite AAU program. "Everyone knew coming in how big he would be to our team, so he knew getting in the weight room would not only help himself but us this year. He knew the guys in the Big Ten were big bodies and he was just going to have to put on some weight so he could handle them."

How did he do it? First things first, he ate. A lot.

"He eats more than anyone I know," Etherington said. ". One time we were at Wee Willies, he got two orders of biscuits and gravy and pancakes, these big ole' pancakes. Everyone told him that he couldn't eat them. He ate them, and he was eating other people's food."

Zeller was always that way, but like so many players with bodies like his, he had trouble keeping weight on. But that changed when Indiana strength and conditioning coach Je'Ney Jackson got a hold of him.

"That's what Coach Jackson takes to heart," Elston said. "Getting guys stronger, getting guys quicker. A lot of protein shakes, a lot of lifting. Cody's been good at staying cool. Sometimes Coach Jackson can get a little annoying even. To have Cody just keep his cool, come in and not complain about putting in a lot of hard work. It's paid off. Fifteen pounds, that's huge for him."

Bulky post men like Ohio State's Jared Sullinger, Michigan State's Derrick Nix, Adreian Payne and Draymond Green and Illinois' Meyers Leonard might've been able to use the 215-pound Zeller as a toothpick, but the 230-pound Zeller had the size to withstand their blows and deliver them, and the extra weight didn't cost him in speed or quickness either. He's considered one of the fastest big men in the country in the transition game, and his skill set would be good enough to make him an NBA lottery pick this season if he went pro. Zeller heads into tonight's NCAA regional semifinal game with Kentucky averaging 15.5 points and 6.5 rebounds per game.

"When he was 15 pounds lighter, he was real good on his feet," Elston said. "But Cody put a lot of the weight into his legs. He still had the quick feet that he always had. Putting him at the five just made him that much more of a force. Hard to stop a man with good feet, good quickness, the jumping ability that he has. It's hard to stop someone like that."

Said Crean: "It's helped him see that he can do different things. He can not only hold up, but he can flourish with a lot of minutes over an extended period of time. Every time that he maybe got a little bit tired this season, he was able to recover from it so quickly because of that mental toughness and because he's in such great shape."

And because Zeller's been able to play in the middle, that allows the Hoosiers to space the whole floor. Using the defensive minded Tom Pritchard in the post last season meant that the only way the Hoosiers were getting points in the paint was if Christian Watford posted up.

Now, even though he's technically a power forward, Watford can play inside and outside and is second to junior guard Jordan Hulls in 3-point shooting. The Hoosiers have three scoring options in the backcourt at all times, and Zeller makes sure they have room to shoot.

He hasn't taken a single 3-pointer this year, but Crean pointed out earlier this season that the Hoosiers went from shooting 34.6 percent from beyond the arc last season to 43.7 percent this season — good for second in Division I and the best in the Big Ten — and that Zeller is a big reason why. Overall they're shooting 49.1 percent from the field, which is sixth in Division I and better than 461 percent last year, and averaging 76.9 points per game, which was a Big Ten best.

"If you think you can guard him one-on-one, go for it," Elston said. "Cody's a real good player, but if you bring the double-team, he's such a great passer. He can pass it out and hit the open guy, and that open guy's going to hit the open shot. Really, he just sets everybody up for an open shot."

And that's how much of a difference 15 pounds makes.

2011-2012 SEASON STATS

	G-GS	MPG	AFG	3PFG	FT	OR-Rebs	AVG.	AST	TO	BLK	STL	AVG.
Cody Zeller	36-36	28.5	200-321	0-0	163-216	87-236	6.6	45	60	42	49	15.6
Christian Watford	36-36	28.4	141-339	52-119	119-146	42-208	5.8	48	62	16	27	12.6
Jordan Hulls	36-36	30.1	143-284	72-146	62-69	10-89	2.5	120	76	2	38	11.7
Victor Oladipo	36-34	26.7	136-289	10-48	108-144	63-191	5.3	73	76	21	49	10.8
Will Sheehey	31-11	22.4	100-198	18-47	50-71	35-97	3.1	33	41	7	15	8.6
Verdell Jones	30-23	24.5	72-172	10-33	71-94	19-87	2.9	95	73	8	21	7.5
Matt Roth	34-0	11.8	44-82	42-77	15-15	5-22	0.6	14	5	1	4	4.3
Derek Elston	34-4	12.3	53-107	16-29	22-38	18-80	2.4	13	22	10	6	4.2
Remy Abell	32-0	8.3	28-63	6-15	33-42	12-30	0.9	15	16	1	6	3.0
Tom Pritchard	36-0	9.9	22-40	0-1	4-9	26-58	1.6	14	10	5	5	1.3
Austin Etherington	16-0	4.8	7-16	2-8	4-5	4-14	0.9	1	2	1	2	1.3
Kory Barnett	16-0	1.5	3-6	1-4	0-2	0-3	0.2	2	1	0	1	0.4
Raphael Smith	9-0	1.3	0-3	0-1	2-2	0-2	0.2	0	2	0	0	0.2
Daniel Moore	21-0	4.6	0-5	0-2	2-3	2-10	0.5	13	9	0	9	0.1
Taylor Wayer	8-0	1.4	0-1	0-1	0-0	0-1	0.1	0	0	0	0	0.0
Jeff Howard	10-0	1.6	0-2	0-0	0-2	2-2	0.2	1	1	1	1	0.0
Total	**36**		**949-1928**	**229-531**	**655-858**	**383-1240**	**34.4**	**487**	**463**	**115**	**233**	**77.3**
Opponents	**36**		**847-1988**	**219-628**	**479-682**	**391-1094**	**30.4**	**376**	**482**	**146**	**241**	**66.4**

2011-2012 SEASON RESULTS

Date	Opponent Location	Result	Leading scorer
11/11/2011	Stony Brook/Assembly Hall	W, 96-66	Zeller/Oladipo 16
11/13/2011	Chattanooga/Assembly Hall	W, 78-53	Oladipo 21
11/16/2011	Evansville/Ford Center	W, 94-73	Jones 17
11/19/2011	Savannah State/Assembly Hall	W, 94-65	Zeller 23
11/21/2011	Gardner-Webb/Assembly Hall	W, 73-49	Sheehey 15
11/27/2011	Butler/Assembly Hall	W, 75-59	Sheehey 21
11/30/2011	N.C. State/RBC Center	W, 86-75	Hulls 20
12/04/2011	Stetson/Assembly Hall	W, 84-50	Zeller 16
12/10/2011	Kentucky/Assembly Hall	W, 73-72	Watford 20
12/17/2011	Notre Dame TV/Bankers Life Fieldhouse	W, 69-58	Zeller 21
12/19/2011	Howard/Assembly Hall	W, 107-50	Hulls 16
12/22/2011	Md.-Baltimore County/Assembly Hall	W, 89-47	Watford 22
12/28/2011	Michigan State/Breslin Center	L, 80-65	Watford 26
12/31/2011	Ohio State/Assembly Hall	W, 74-70	Hulls 17
01/05/2012	Michigan/Assembly Hall	W, 73-71	Watford 25
01/08/2012	Penn State/Bryce Jordan Center	W, 88-82	Hulls 28
01/12/2012	Minnesota/Assembly Hall	L, 77-74	Zeller 23
01/15/2012	Ohio State/Value City Arena	L, 80-63	Zeller 16
01/18/2012	Nebraska/DeVaney Sports Center	L, 70-69	Zeller 18
01/22/2012	Penn State/Assembly Hall	W, 73-54	Zeller 18
01/26/2012	Wisconsin/Kohl Center	L, 57-50	Watford/Jones 12
01/29/2012	Iowa/Assembly Hall	W, 103-89	Zeller 26
02/01/2012	Michigan/Crisler Arena	L, 68-56	Hulls 18
02/04/2012	Purdue/Mackey Arena	W, 78-61	Oladipo 23
02/09/2012	Illinois/Assembly Hall	W, 84-71	Zeller 22
02/15/2012	Northwestern/Assembly Hall	W, 71-66	Zeller 23
02/19/2012	Iowa/Carver-Hawkeye Arena	L, 78-66	Zeller/Oladipo 15
02/22/2012	North Carolina Central/Assembly Hall	W, 75-56	Zeller 17
02/26/2012	Minnesota/Williams Arena	W, 69-50	Watford/Hulls/Oladipo 12
02/28/2012	Michigan State/Assembly Hall	W, 70-55	Zeller 18
03/04/2012	Purdue/Assembly Hall	W, 85-74	Watford 19
Big Ten Tournament			
03/08/2012	Penn State/Bankers Life Fieldhouse	W, 75-58	Hulls 20
03/09/2012	Wisconsin/Bankers Life Fieldhouse	L, 79-71	Watford/Zeller/Hulls 17
NCAA Tournament			
03/15/2012	New Mexico State/Rose Garden	W, 79-66	Hulls 22
03/17/2012	Va. Commonwealth/Rose Garden	W, 63-61	Zeller/Watford 16
03/23/2012	Kentucky/Georgia Dome	L, 102-90	Watford 27

from the
Cook family of employees
to our IU Basketball family

CONGRATULATIONS
on a great season!

Cook Medical | Cook Group | Cook Pharmica | CFC Properties

COOK HALL

THANKS

for a 'Sweet' Season!

Indiana University men's basketball is back. Coach Tom Crean and the
Indiana Hoosiers took their winning ways straight to the NCAA's Sweet Sixteen,
igniting the Hoosier Nation in support of their team. On and off the court,
our players showed integrity and dedication, the true spirit of IU.

Thanks for the memories—we're ready for next year!

INDIANA UNIVERSITY
BLOOMINGTON

INDIANA UNIVERSITY
FOUNDATION

INDIANA UNIVERSITY
ALUMNI ASSOCIATION

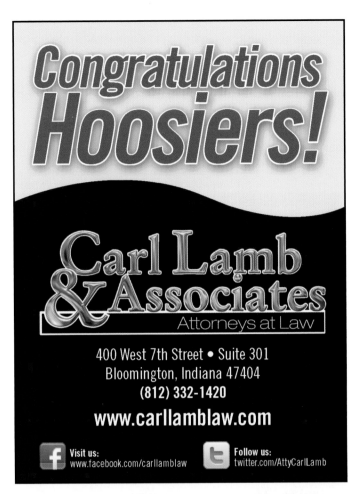